How to be Successful in

Civil Services

HOW TO BECOME

IAS-IPS?

How to be Successful in

Civil Services

HOW TO BECOME

IAS-IPS?

Deepak Anand, IAS

Foreword

Dr. D.N. Gautam, IPS

Former DGP, Bihar

PRABHAT

PRAKASHAN

Published by
PRABHAT PRAKASHAN PVT. LTD.
4/19 Asaf Ali Road,
New Delhi-110002 (INDIA)
e-mail: prabhatbooks@gmail.com

ISBN 978-93-5521-794-3
HOW TO BE SUCCESSFUL IN CIVIL SERVICES-HOW TO BECOME IAS-IPS?
by Deepak Anand, IAS

Edition
2026

Price
₹ 375 (Rupees Three Hundred Seventy Five Only)

Printed at
R-Tech Offset Printers, Delhi

This book is dedicated to my
Father Late Padam Shankar Chaudhary and
Mother Smt. Malti Devi.

Foreword

'How to be Successful in Civil Services— How to Become IAS-IPS?' is a product of its author Deepak Anand's firsthand experience in attempting and succeeding in Civil Services Examinations. It is quite pleasing that he honoured his hard work by this book after getting with the prestigious Indian Administrative Service and translated the same into social action by taking up to groom youngsters for the same in the remote Banka district of Bihar State while creditably performing his duties as collector and District Magistrate of Banka. He is continuing his social service even after being shifted from the District to a secretariat job at Patna.

The Union Public Service Commission has been experimenting with the Civil Services Examinations as their labours are not being complimented by the reports from the field about their selectees. The so called toughest examination of India would yield such a servile crop of civil servants as we have been witnessing and their alleged brilliance bowing before the species of political masters they look down upon more often than not raises deep issues that call for urgent attentions. Not reforms but a fresh new glance is needed. I apprehend that the servility of Civil Servants may be directly connected with what the preparations for the Civil Service Examinations do to the mind-culture of the candidates. I got this clue while going through the book 'Care of the Soul' by philosopher Thomas Moore. Psychological testing of the tests itself is an area that should no longer remain alien to our education system. All examinations must be considered education in itself.

I wish civil services aspirants benefit from Deepak Anand's good work and for Deepak Anand to keep his practice of writing work. I also pray that someday Indians will get the Civil Service they deserve and the various Governments both at the Centre and States to realize that their currents pre-occupations with the Power-Politics is not making India any better place for their grand-children. My verdict on the Civil Service for the present is that what is being considered the best is not turning out good enough. I wish to be proved wrong.

–Dr. D.N. Gautam, IPS
Former DGP, Bihar

Why This Book?

Accountability, responsibility and discipline are the three most important guiding principles in life. I have followed these three principles with earnestness since the time I came to my senses. That is the reason I have always been a dedicated student and have done well in my examinations. While doing my graduation, I always dreamt of doing something worthwhile in life and I was yearning to do something for my country. It was, thus, only natural that I was inclined towards the Civil Services. On enquiry, I came to know that this profession offers an opportunity to serve the country and its people. Primarily, it dealt with the common man's day-to-day problems. It was a profession which made a person accountable as well as responsible.

These qualities of the Civil Service fascinated me and I started preparing to qualify for it. The preparations for the examination are no less than a venture. Once you have begun, there is no turning back. If you stick to your aim, you are bound to succeed and this success, cannot be taken away from you. However, in order to succeed it is important that you follow the aforesaid three principles.

I began my preparations with full vigour. Like Arjun in the Mahabharata, my aim was to hit the 'eye of the fish'. I cleared the preliminaries and turned my attention to the main examination and cleared that too. Thereafter, I successfully answered all the difficult questions during the interview and finally reached my destination. I obtained 225 marks out of 300 in the interview, which were the highest marks in Hindi medium.

I strongly suggest that you do not consider the interviewers lightly or consider them as Gods. Even the best of candidates, who clear the 'Preliminary' and the 'Main' examinations, fail in the 'Interview'. So, consider the 'Interview' as a *chakravyuh* (maze), which is difficult to get through, as I did. Prepare for it with patience, wisdom, understanding and answer all the questions with a smile to emerge victorious.

In this book, I have tried to share some of my experiences. In no way am I suggesting that this book is comprehensive. It is a small effort to acquaint aspirants with some of my experiences. It is my belief that if you have studied honestly till your graduation and have done well in your examinations over the years, and have also kept yourself abreast of current affairs, it is quite possible that you may not have to do any special preparations. Remember, the civil servants are persons like us. So, you can also become a civil servant, assume the responsibility of serving your country and live respectfully.

My best wishes for a successful career in the Civil Services.

Yours,

—Deepak Anand, IAS.

Introduction

The Civil Services are immensely respected in our country. Countless candidates aspire to get selected in the examinations in order to serve the country, make a name and make their family proud. Countless students take the examinations every year, but only a few make it through. Some miss the chance by a mark or two and are left with no choice but to retry next year.

Actually, if the aspirants receive proper guidance, their chances of success brighten considerably. Most aspirants are blindly dependent on the coaching centres which 'guarantee' success in the examinations. I am of the view that instead of running after such coaching institutes, if one depends more on the reliable study material, it would prove more beneficial. I got an opportunity to go through the book Deepak Anandji has written for the Civil Services aspirants. I want to congratulate him for bringing his years of experience in a nutshell which fills a major void in expert guidance in this regard.

Deepak Anandji hails from a middle-class family and has risen to the position of district magistrate by dint of hard work and dedication. Anandji himself faced small hindrances in the way of becoming a Civil Servant and has dealt with such problems in this book, offering solutions on how to overcome them. I am sure this book will prove to be a milestone in the preparations for the Civil Services Examination.

In this book, Anandji has dealt with all the three stages, namely Preliminary, Main and Interview in an easy and interesting manner. I am confident that if you read this book, it will make your journey in dealing with the examination a lot easier.

I once again congratulate Anandji for writing this book and hope it continues to guide and groom the aspirants for the Civil Services in the years to come.

With best wishes,

—Anand Kumar, Super 30

Contents

Indian Administrative Service: An Introduction

My administrative decisions will find appreciation 50 years from now. I shall no longer be alive then to witness them.

—George Bush (Former US President)

The Civil Services are considered as the backbone of Indian administrative system and have the glamour and status that make it a dream profession for the countless youth of the country.

Whenever an educated Indian youth thinks of a job, three factors, namely designation, status and stability determine his choice. If there is one profession that can ensure all three, it is the Civil Services. It is this established service that attracts the ambitious, the capable and those who are willing to accept challenges. This is the only profession that strikes a balance between personal ambitions and an opportunity to serve the country. This is the reason that many forsake the other options like medicine and engineering to try their luck in this profession.

The profession offers the opportunity to deal with innumerable responsible and challenging tasks, which no other career offers. The diversity of work it offers is also its speciality.

Administrative Set-up

All departments of the government (other than the armed forces) come under the Indian Civil Services which are categorised into Central and State levels. The officials for the Central services are selected by the Union Public Service

Commission (UPSC) and those for the State level are selected by the respective state public service commissions. The Central Civil Services are divided into two categories, namely All-India Services and Central Services. The Indian Administrative Service, Police Services and Indian Forest Services are all-India services, which come under the purview of both the Central and State governments.

Selection Process

The Union Public Service Commission (UPSC) conducts an all-India examination every year, which is called 'Civil Services Examination'. This examination is held in three phases: Preliminary, Main and Interview. The 'Preliminary' is a screening test, which is objective and optional in nature. The 'Main' is a written examination which tests a candidate's depth and analytical skills. The final stage is the 'Interview' which tests a candidate's personality traits and awareness of general affairs.

1. Preliminary Examinations: This is the first important step in the selection. This is primarily a screening test to weed out those candidates who are not serious about the examinations. The pattern of the first paper has been altered. Now, there is no test of optional topics. In its place, there are two objective-type question papers. The question papers are of 200 marks each, totalling to 400 marks. Both the objective-type question papers are the same for all the students. While the earlier system laid more stress on a candidate's extent of knowledge in a subject, the new system lays more emphasis on his aptitude. The first paper is of General Studies which has questions related to current affairs of national and international importance, India's history and national movements, geography of India and the world, India's political system and administration, financial and social development, environment and ecology and general science. The second paper lays emphasis on comprehension and communication skills, interpersonal and logical capabilities, general aptitude, and data analysis.

Negative Marking: In the first paper, negative marking has been introduced. For a wrong answer, one-third of the marks that the question carries is deducted. If a candidate gives more than one answer to a question, it is considered incorrect.

2. Main Examinations: This is a very important stage of the examination as it carries 2,025 marks, which prove decisive in ensuring success. The marks obtained in the main examination (written) and the interview are added together to arrive at the final result which forms the basis and determines a candidate's All India Rank. The written examination (Main) has the following question papers:

Qualifying Paper (A) - 300 marks : This examination is taken on one of the languages chosen by a candidate out of the languages contained in the Eighth Schedule of the Constitution. For example, if Hindi is the mother-tongue of a candidate, then he/she can choose Hindi. In the same manner, candidates can choose as per their preference of the languages like Bengali, Punjabi, Guajarati etc. This paper of the Indian languages is not applicable to the candidates, who come from Arunachal Pradesh, Manipur, Meghalaya, Mizoram, Nagaland and Sikkim.

Qualifying Paper (B) - English : This paper is compulsory for all and the paper shall be taken in English only. This also contains 300 marks.

The qualifying papers of the Indian language (A) and English (B) will be of matriculation or equivalent level in which out of 300 marks, scoring 75 marks are compulsory for qualifying each of the paper—(A) and (B).

Marks obtained in both these question papers will not give any weightage to determine the qualifying ranks in the main examination.

The assessment of all the candidates shall be done on the basis of their performance in question papers of Essay, General Studies and the optional paper simultaneously with their performance in the qualifying question papers of the Indian language and English. But, the performance in respect of Essay, General Studies and the optional subject shall be looked into, of only those candidates who obtain, as the minimum qualifying standard, 25 per cent marks in the Indian language and also 25 per cent marks in English.

The calculation of marks obtained by the candidates in Paper I-VII only shall be done for giving them a place in the merit list. The Commission reserves the right to determine the qualifying marks of any or all the question papers of the Examination.

Compulsory Question Paper

Qualifying paper – (A) **300 marks**

Chosen by a candidate out of the languages contained in the Eighth Schedule of the Constitution. This paper is not applicable to the candidate belonging to the North-East Area.

Qualifying Paper – (B) **300 marks**

English

Compulsory for all.

Question Paper – I

Essay 250 marks

Question Paper – II

General Studies – I 250 marks

(Indian Tradition and Culture, World History and Geography and Society)

Question Paper – III

General Studies – II 250 marks

(Form of governance, Constitution, System of Governance, Social Justice and International Relations)

Question Paper – IV

General Studies – III 250 marks

(Technology, Economic Development, Biodiversity, Environmental Safety and Disaster Management)

Question Paper – V

General Studies – IV 250 marks

(Ethics, Integrity and Aptitude)

Question Paper – VI	
Optional Subject Question Paper – I	250 marks
Question Paper – VII	
Optional Subject Question Paper – II	250 marks
SUB-TOTAL (Written Examination)	1,750 marks
Personality Test	275 marks
TOTAL MARKS	2,025 marks

3. Interview: This is the last but very important stage of the examination. The intention here is not as much to judge the extent of knowledge as it is to determine one's values, strengths of personality and awareness of one's surroundings. This carries **275 marks**. It is necessary that you have a balanced personality and views. The board is usually impressed with a candidate's honesty, openness, awareness and gentle personality traits.

Opportunity to Serve

An efficient administrative system is essential for a country's development. Challenges are part of a Civil Servant's daily affairs and that is the reason it is a profession of the highest order and respect in India.

Due to its being an elite service, there are challenges associated with this profession which make it more attractive and stable. Under the Constitution, the services give one the authority to serve the country and its people. The profession is stable and with fewer uncertainties.

Role of Coaching Centres

They play a supporting role. They can polish your personality, but depending entirely on coaching is not enough for the civil services examination preparation.

The Post-Covid Scenario

After Covid-19, there is a new hypothesis of online classes which has emerged before the organisations in education sector. In the midst of this crisis of about two year's duration, different organisations in the Education sector are organising their classes in hybrid mode (online/offline). The online classes have their own negative and positive aspects, but the examination system of the Union Public Service Commission is an offline exercise even today. For this reason, it seems more logical for the candidates that they should prepare for the examination with offline medium in line with the current situation. If we look at it correctly, the main examination is a completely written examination, where you need a guide or a teacher for evaluation of your answers.

Medium of Examination

Since the introduction of CSAT, it has become compulsory for students of the Hindi medium to study English. However, it is not true that only those proficient in English can be successful in the Civil Services Examination. This perception has gained ground because most of the study material is in English. Several candidates, who have followed the Hindi medium of instruction, have recently succeeded in clearing the examination with flying colours.

In recent years, the result of Hindi medium has shown a decline when compared to English medium. However, in respect of 2021 Examination, there are some good rankings also from the Hindi medium candidates. The main reason why the candidates of Hindi medium got a lesser result is that they could not clear the CSAT question paper. In the last two-three years, the nature of CSAT question paper has undergone a change and it has become very exhaustive.

Despite scoring good marks in the first question paper, the Hindi medium candidates could not perform very well in CSAT question paper thus failing to get eligible for the main examination. This was contrary to the expectation.

Qualifications

Only Indian citizens are qualified to apply for the Indian Administrative and Police Services. For other services, Nepalese,

Bhutanese and Tibetans, who have settled in India prior to 1962, are also eligible to apply. Candidates have to be graduates or its equivalent from a university recognised by the Central or State governments or the UGC. Those in the final year of graduation can apply, but they would be required to submit their marksheets of having passed the examination before taking the Main Civil Services Examination.

For administrative services, a candidate must be between 21 and 32 years of age, both being the minimum and maximum age limits. Various concessions have been granted in different categories, particularly to the candidates belonging to the scheduled castes and scheduled tribes.

Eligibility

Besides, a person of the Indian origin who has come to India, for living here permanently from Pakistan, Burma, Srilanka, Eastern African countries-Kenya, Uganda, Tanzania, Zambia, Malawi, Zaire, Ethiopia and Vietnam, after immigration.

The Minimum Educational Qualification for Making Application

A candidate must possess a degree of graduation or its equivalent from a University approved by the Central government of India, or a State government constituted by a State Legislative assembly, or the University Grant Commission. A candidate appearing for the last year's examination of such graduation or equivalent examination can also apply. But he/she will have to produce a certificate of passing the graduation or its equivalent examination before appearing in the main Examination.

Age Limit/Number of Chances

A candidate should be 21 years of age on the first of August of the year's examination for which he/she wishes to appear. For example, a candidate should be 21 years of age as on August 1, 2022.

Category	Age Limit	Number of chances
General	21 to 32 years	6
Other Backward Classes	21 to 35 years	9
Scheduled Caste/Tribe	21 to 37 years	No Limit

Appearing for the preliminary examination shall be reckoned as one chance of appearing in Civil Services Examination.

How to Apply

The candidates can apply online by using the website https://upsconline.nic.in. The detailed instructions for applying online are available on the above mentioned website.

The candidate must possess the details of his/her any one photo IDs like Aadhar Card, Voter's ID Card, PAN Card, Passport, Driving License or any other photo ID issued by State/ Central government, which he/she will have to make available while filling up his/her online application form. The candidate will have to scan a copy of his/her photo ID, the details of which have been given by him/her in his/her online application, and upload it. This photo ID shall be used in all future references.

Examination Fee

There is no fee for scheduled caste/scheduled tribe candidates, women or the physically-challenged.

The aspirants must get fully engaged in their preparations once they have acquired their graduate degree. The Union Public Service Commission usually declares the date of the Preliminary Examination in February.

❑

Posts and Authority

The ability to touch the heart of others and the magic to endear them depicts the entirety and characteristics of talent.

—Rabindranath Tagore

The Civil Services are a gift from France to the world. In India, they were introduced by the British in 1885. During the British Raj in India, officers of the Civil Services had enormous powers as they were expected to maintain law and order and collect taxes. Today, the Civil Services operate in a democratic set-up where their main intention is to ensure development and progress.

If we talk about posts, politicians have been given the highest posts in India, followed by the secretaries, who are Indian Administrative Service (IAS) officers. If the Prime Minister or minister occupies the highest position, then the second position is occupied by the Civil Servant.

The Indian Administrative Service (IAS) has emerged from the Indian Civil Service (ICS). To keep the memory of ICS and Indian Police (IP) alive, the government created their equivalents namely, IAS and IPS. The difference is that the earlier two were the brainchildren of the British Raj, while the latter two were created by the first government of independent India.

As democracy evolved in independent India, the Civil Services gained in prominence. Formulating policies and decision-making moved in the hands of elected representatives. The Civil Services continued to give advice fearlessly and, with time, the dedication of the officials ensured all-round progress and development. The need of the hour was to create new equations between the politicians and the Civil Services Officers, which could ensure smooth functioning and this was achieved in 1967.

In policy matters, the Civil Services Officers have an important role to play. According to Articles 77 and 166 of the Constitution, for the governance at the Central and State levels, the secretaries of the ministries and departments are expected to implement certain rules. Even if a minister orders something in variance with the rules, it is the duty of the secretary to point it out to him. If the minister still does not comply with the rules, the secretary is empowered to send a file to this effect to the Prime Minister or the Chief Minister, whichever is applicable. Section 14 of the Constitution empowers the Civil Services to initiate an investigation against them, a power which no other Civil Services in the world have. Even our own Armed Forces do not have such a power. Article 312 of the Constitution gives the all-India services massive powers. In return, the country wants the Civil Services Officers to dispense their responsibilities without corrupt practices, advise our elected representatives fearlessly, carry out their duties with dedication and impartiality, upgrade their professional expertise and serve the people selflessly.

Responsibilities of a Civil Servant

An IAS officer is not only a policy-maker, but is also responsible for implementation of the policies. He represents the government in different countries and on international platforms. He is empowered to sign pacts on behalf of the government. When he works on the district level, he is known as District Magistrate and Collector, among other names. He is directly responsible for all the work undertaken in the district, be it developmental work, law and order or emergency services. He serves in various capacities as Chief Secretary, Principal Secretary, among others in the Secretariats. The highest post as an IAS officer is the Prime Minister's or Chief Minister's Principal Secretary.

Indian Police Service (IPS)

An IPS officer gets his first appointment as a Superintendent or Commissioner of Police. He is responsible for ensuring safety of the people, maintaining law and order, crime control and traffic control, among other duties. In addition, he renders his services to other Central police organisations like the CBI, RPF and BSF. The highest designation as an IPS officer is that of an Inspector General of a State or the Director of the CBI or IB.

Indian Foreign Service (IFS)

An IFS officer manages different duties like diplomacy, trade and cultural exchanges. He is involved in framing the country's foreign policies and their implementation. As an IFS officer, the highest designation is that of Ambassador or Foreign Secretary.

State Civil Services

The State Civil Services officials are responsible for resolving problems at the Divisional or Tehsil levels. The officials are known as SDMs or SDOs in different states. D.S.P., Excise officers and BDOs are also part of the State Civil Services. The officials are selected through the examinations conducted by the State Civil Services.

Spearheading nation-building

In order to ensure ideal governance, the Constitution of India gives immense powers to the Civil Services officers. For implementing any developmental plan or handling any issue involving public welfare or for resolving any emergency situation of the gravest proportion, the first initiative comes from the administration. So, it will not be an exaggeration to say that the development of a country happens due to an able and efficient administration.

Self-satisfaction

There have been occasions when we have seen people grappling with problems and hardship. Our hearts have cried out for them. We have all asked the same question at some point in our lives—How can we resolve these problems? The Indian Administrative Services hold the key to resolving these problems. Working as Civil Servants, they can use all the powers given to them to alleviate the woes of the people. The self-satisfaction thus earned in helping out others is unparalleled, which no other service provides.

❑

3

Examination Framework

The acknowledgement of ignorance,
is a big step towards gaining knowledge.

—Acharya Sriram Sharma

The administrative services are considered as the most prestigious services in India, given the accountability and responsibility that come with them. That is the reason that countless youth are attracted towards them every year.

The administrative services are the country's most prestigious services. The officials are given immense powers. There is official authority and social responsibility in this profession, as the services are associated with running the country smoothly. Being associated with the services is a dream for the youth as it accords their family great respectability in the society.

The examinations for the administrative services are conducted by the Union Public Service Commission (UPSC) and the details are announced in the newspapers from time to time. The examinations are carefully and meticulously organised and leave no room for shortcomings.

Selecting the Subjects

Students from the general category can take the Civil Services Examinations four times. The examinee becomes a far more knowledgeable man due to the hard work he puts into its preparations. The preparations are very tough and one needs undivided concentration to get through. Moreover, while preparing for the Preliminary examination, one must keep the Main examination in mind too. It must be emphasised that judicious selection of subjects can make or mar the prospects of an examinee. The subjects must be of interest to him/her. Most examinees choose the subjects they have studied for their Honours Course. However, one can choose other subjects also. The only thing one needs to keep in mind is that we have sufficient knowledge and interest in whichever subject we choose.

The following posts are filled through the Civil Services examination:

(i) Indian Administrative Service
(ii) Indian Foreign Service
(iii) Indian Police Service
(iv) Indian Audit and Accounts Service, Group 'A'
(v) Indian Civil Accounts Service, Group 'A'
(vi) Indian Corporate Law Service, Group 'A'
(vii) Indian Defence Accounts Service, Group 'A'
(viii) Indian Defence Estates Service, Group 'A' (ix) Indian Information Service, Group 'A'
(x) Indian Postal Service, Group 'A'
(xi) Indian P&T Accounts and Finance Service, Group 'A'
(xii) Indian Railway Protection Force Service, Group 'A'
(xiii) Indian Revenue Service (Customs & Indirect Taxes) Group 'A'
(xiv) Indian Revenue Service (Income Tax) Group 'A'
(xv) Indian Trade Service, Group 'A' (Grade III)
(xvi) Indian Railway Management Service, Group 'A'
(xvii) Armed Forces Headquarters Civil Service, Group 'B' (Section Officer's Grade)
(xviii) Delhi, Andaman and Nicobar Islands, Lakshadweep, Daman & Diu and Dadra & Nagar Haveli Civil Service (DANICS), Group 'B'
(xix) Delhi, Andaman and Nicobar Islands, Lakshadweep, Daman & Diu and Dadra & Nagar Haveli Police Service (DANIPS), Group 'B'
(xx) Pondicherry Civil Service (PONDICS), Group 'B'
(xxi) Pondicherry Police Service (PONDIPS), Group 'B'

The selected IAS and IPS officers have to begin working at the district level. This is the grooming period for the officers as they come in touch with the ground realities and start taking up responsibilities. Gradually, they are promoted to higher ranks. In all, the power, responsibility, accountability and respectability, along with the self-satisfaction make this profession the most sought after in the country.

As per the Civil Service Examination Notification No. 05/2022 dated .....issued last year, a notification about a total of 19 services was issued in which the total number of posts determined was 861. Thereafter, Department of Personnel and Training has decided about recruiting 150 officers of the Indian Railways Administration Service Group 'A' through the recruitment process of the civil services examination 2022, and the total number of posts are now 1011 instead of 861.

The Ministry of Railways issued a separate Notification on December 02, 2022 in respect of the Indian Railways Management Service, wherein 150 posts were announced for the service examination from the year 2023; in addition to it, the Notice also mentioned that the preliminary examination for the Indian Railways Management Service shall be taken through the Civil Services (Preliminary) Examination only. It is like the same for which examination for the Indian Forest Service is being conducted. After passing the preliminary examination only on the basis of the subjects for the main Civil Services Examination, the main examination for the Indian Railways Management Service shall be taken and for this, a separate interview process was talked about, but at present, in the Notification published by the UPSC for the Civil Services Examination 2023, the Indian Railways Management Service has again been included in that.

Year	Number of posts
2017	980
2018	782
2019	806
2020	796
2021	712
2022	1011
2023	1105

If we look at the total number of posts declared in the civil services examination during the last few years, we find that the Union Public Service Commission has declared the maximum 1105 posts for this year (2023).

Section-I

Planning for the Examinations

This competitive examination has two successive steps:

For the selection of candidates who qualify to appear for the Main examination—the Preliminary examination (Objective type).

1. For selection to different services and posts—the Main examination (Written and Interview).

2. The Preliminary examination will have two question papers (multiple-choice objective type) and the topics in Section II (Sub-section A) will carry a maximum of 400 marks. This is only a pre-qualification examination and the marks obtained in this examination by those who qualify to appear for the Main examination are not counted for their final selection. The number of candidates allowed to take the Main examination will be 12-13 times the number of total vacancies in various posts in that particular year. Only those candidates who clear the Preliminary examination in a particular year will be allowed to take the Main examinations in that year.

3. Those candidates who secure the minimum qualifying marks in the Main examination will, according to Section-II (Sub-section C), be called for an Interview. The marks secured in this examination will be added to determine the rank. The number of candidates called for the Interview will be approximately double the number of vacancies. The final ranking will be done by adding the marks obtained in the written examination and the interview. Appointment to various services and posts will be done based on the rank obtained by the candidates.

Section-II

Format of the Preliminary and Main examinations and Subjects:

A. Preliminary Examination

There will be two question papers, both compulsory and carrying 200 marks each.

Question Paper-I (200 marks); Time: Two hours

Important national and international current events

History of India and Indian National Movement

India and World Geography - India and World natural, social and financial geography

Indian polity and governance - Constitution, political system, Panchayati Raj, public policies and issues related to rights, among other topics

Financial and Social Development – All-round development, poverty, inclusion, census and social issues, among others

Issues related to environmental concerns, animals and organisms and climatic conditions, among other topics

General Science

Question Paper-II (200 marks); Time: Two hours

Comprehension

Communication and interpersonal skills

Logical and analytical skills

Decision-making and problems' resolution

General IQ

Fundamental statistics (numbers and their relation, series expansion, among others, all of class X level), interpretation of data (chart, graph and index, adequacy of data among others, all of class X level)

English language proficiency (of class X level).

Remark-1 : Proficiency in English language of class X level (last item in Question Paper-II) will be tested and the answers must be given through examples in

English language only. No translation will be provided.

Remark-2 : All questions will be of objective type with multiple choices.

Remark-3 : To qualify, it is mandatory that the candidate attempts both the preliminary examination question papers. If a candidate attempts only one paper, he will be deemed disqualified.

Notes:

1. Both question papers will be of objective type with multiple choices.
2. The question papers will be both in Hindi and English. However, the English language question paper (last item of Question Paper-II) must be answered in English with examples also in English. No translation will be provided.
3. Both the question papers will be of 2 hours duration.
4. Visually-impaired candidates will be given extra time of 20 minutes for each paper.

B. Main Examination

The main Examination is intended to assess the overall intellectual traits and depth of understanding of candidates rather than merely the range of their information and memory.

The nature and standard of questions in the General Studies papers (Paper II to Paper V) will be such that a well-educated person will be able to answer them without any specialised study. The questions will be such as to test a candidate's general awareness of a variety of subjects, which will have relevance for a career in Civil Services. The questions are likely to test the candidate's basic understanding of all relevant issues, and ability to analyse, and take a view on conflicting socio-economic goals, objectives and demands. The candidates must give relevant, meaningful and succinct answers.

The scope of the syllabus for optional subject papers (Paper VI and Paper VII) for the examination is broadly of the honours degree level i.e. a level higher than the bachelors' degree and lower than the masters' degree. In the case of Engineering,

Medical Science and law, the level corresponds to the bachelors' degree.

Syllabi of the papers included in the scheme of Civil Services (Main) Examination are given as follows :—

Qualifying Papers on Indian Languages and English

The aim of the paper is to test the candidates' ability to read and understand serious discursive prose,

The pattern of questions would be broadly as follows :

(i) Comprehension of given passages.
(ii) Precis Writing.
(iii) Usage and Vocabulary.
(iv) Short Essays.

Indian Languages :—

(i) comprehension of given passages.
(ii) Precis Writing.
(iii) Usage and Vocabulary.
(iv) Short Essays.
(v) Translation from English to the Indian Language and vice-versa.

Note 1 : The papers on Indian Languages and English will be of Matriculation or equivalent standard and will be of qualifying nature only. The marks obtained in these papers will not be counted for ranking.

Note 2 : The candidates will have to answer the English and Indian Languages papers in English and the respective Indian language (except where translation is involved).

Paper-I

Essay: Candidates may be required to write essays on multiple topics. They will be expected to keep closely to the subject of the essay to arrange their ideas in orderly fashion, and to write concisely. Credit will be given for effective and exact expression.

Paper-II

General Studies-I: Indian Heritage and Culture, History and Geography of the World and Society

- Indian culture will cover the salient aspects of Art Forms, Literature and Architecture from ancient to modern times.
- Modern Indian history from about the middle of the eighteenth century until the present—significant events, personalities, issues.
- The Freedom Struggle—its various stages and important contributors/contributions from different parts of the country.
- Post-independence consolidation and reorganisation within the country.
- History of the world will include events from 18th century such as industrial revolution, world wars, redrawal of national boundaries, colonisation, decolonisation, political philosophies like communism, capitalism, socialism etc.—their forms and effect on the society.
- Salient features of Indian Society, Diversity of India.
- Role of women and women's organisation, population and associated issues, poverty and developmental issues, urbanisation, their problems and their remedies.
- Effects of globalisation on Indian society.
- Social empowerment, communalism, regionalism & secularism.
- Salient features of world's physical geography.
- Distribution of key natural resources across the world (including South Asia and the Indian sub-continent); factors responsible for the location of primary, secondary, and tertiary sector industries in various parts of the world (including India).
- Important Geophysical phenomena such as earthquakes, Tsunami, Volcanic activity, cyclone etc., geographical features and their location, changes in critical geographical features (including water-bodies and ice-caps) and in flora and fauna and the effects of such changes.

Paper-III

General Studies-II: Governance, Constitution, Polity, Social Justice and International relations

- Indian Constitution—historical underpinnings, evolution, features, amendments, significant provisions and basic structure.
- Functions and responsibilities of the Union and the States, issues and challenges pertaining to the federal structure, devolution of powers and finances up to local levels and challenges therein.
- Separation of powers between various organs dispute redressal mechanisms and institutions.
- Comparison of the Indian constitutional scheme with that of other countries.
- Parliament and State legislatures—structure, functioning, conduct of business, powers & privileges and issues arising out of these.
- Structure, organisation and functioning of the Executive and the Judiciary—Ministries and Departments of the Government; pressure groups and formal/informal associations and their role in the Polity.
- Salient features of the Representation of People's Act.
- Appointment to various Constitutional posts, powers, functions and responsibilities of various Constitutional Bodies.
- Statutory, regulatory and various quasi-judicial bodies.
- Government policies and interventions for development in various sectors and issues arising out of their design and implementation.
- Development processes and the development industry — the role of NGOs, SHGs, various groups and associations, donors, charities, institutional and other stakeholders.
- Welfare schemes for vulnerable sections of the population by the Centre and States and the performance of these schemes; mechanisms, laws, institutions and Bodies constituted for the protection and betterment of these vulnerable sections.
- Issues relating to development and management of Social Sector/Services relating to Health, Education, Human Resources.
- Issues relating to poverty and hunger.
- Important aspects of governance, transparency and

accountability, e-governance applications, models, successes, limitations, and potential; citizens charters, transparency & accountability and institutional and other measures.

- Role of civil services in a democracy.
- India and its neighborhood-relations.
- Bilateral, regional and global groupings and agreements involving India and/or affecting India's interests.
- Effect of policies and politics of developed and developing countries on India's interests, Indian diaspora.
- Important International institutions, agencies and fora—their structure, mandate.

Paper-IV

General Studies-III: Technology, Economic Development, Bio diversity, Environment, Security and Disaster Management

- Indian Economy and issues relating to planning, mobilisation, of resources, growth, development and employment.
- Inclusive growth and issues arising from it.
- Government Budgeting.
- Major crops—cropping patterns in various parts of the country—different types of irrigation and irrigation systems storage, transport and marketing of agricultural produce and issues and related constraints; e-technology in the aid of farmers.
- Issues related to direct and indirect farm subsidies and minimum support prices; Public Distribution System—objectives, functioning, limitations, and revamping; issues of buffer stocks and food security; Technology missions; economics of animal-rearing.
- Food processing and related industries in India—scope and significance, location, upstream and downstream requirements, supply chain management.
- Land reforms in India.
- Effects of liberalisation on the economy, changes in industrial policy and their effects on industrial growth.
- Infrastructure: Energy, Ports, Roads, Airports, Railways etc.
- Investment models.

- Science and Technology—developments and their applications and effects in everyday life.
- Achievements of Indians in science & technology; indigenisation of technology and developing new technology.
- Awareness in the fields of IT, Space, Computers, robotics, nano-technology, bio-technology and issues relating to intellectual property rights.
- Conservation, environmental pollution and degradation, environmental impact assessment.
- Disaster and disaster management.
- Linkages between development and spread of extremism.
- Role of external state and non-state actors in creating challenges to internal security.
- Challenges to internal security through communication networks, role of media and social networking sites in internal security challenges, basics of cyber security; money-laundering and its prevention.
- Security challenges and their management in border areas—linkages of organised crime with terrorism.
- Various Security forces and agencies and their mandate.

Paper-V

General Studies-IV: Ethics, Integrity and Aptitude

- This paper will include questions to test the candidates' attitude and approach to issues relating to integrity, probity in public life and his problem solving approach to various issues and conflicts faced by him in dealing with society. Questions may utilise the case study approach to determine these aspects. The following broad areas will be covered:
  - Ethics and Human Interface: Essence, determinants and consequences of Ethics in-human actions; dimensions of ethics; ethics—in private and public relationships. Human Values—lessons from the lives and teachings of great leaders, reformers and administrators; role of family society and educational institutions in inculcating values.
  - Attitude: Content, structure, function; its influence and relation with thought and behaviour; moral and political attitudes; social influence and persuasion.
  - Aptitude and foundational values for Civil Service, integrity, impartiality and non-partisanship, objectivity,

dedication to public service, empathy, tolerance and compassion towards the weaker-sections.

- Emotional intelligence—concepts, and their utilities and application in administration and governance.
- Contributions of moral thinkers and philosophers from India and world.
- Public/Civil service values and Ethics in Public administration: Status and problems; ethical concerns and dilemmas in government and private institutions; laws, rules, regulations and conscience as sources of ethical guidance; accountability and ethical governance; strengthening of ethical and moral values in governance; ethical issues in international relations and funding; corporate governance.
- Probity in Governance: Concept of public service; Philosophical basis of governance and probity; Information sharing and transparency in government, Right to Information, Codes of Ethics, Codes of Conduct, Citizen's Charters, Work culture, Quality of service delivery, Utilisation of public funds, challenges of corruption.
- Case Studies on above issues.

List of Optional Subjects for the Main Examination

Group-1

1. Agricultural Science
2. Animal Husbandry and Animal Treatment Science
3. Anthropology
4. Botany
5. Chemistry
6. Civil Engineering
7. Commerce and Accounting
8. Economics
9. Electrical Engineering
10. Geography
11. Geology

12. History
13. Law
14. Management
15. Mathematics
16. Mechanical Engineering
17. Medical Science
18. Philosophy
19. Physics
20. Political Science and International Relations
21. Psychology
22. Public Administration
23. Sociology
24. Statistics
25. Zoology

Group-2

Any one of these Literatures:

Assamese, Bengali, Bodo, Dogri, Gujarati, Hindi, Kannada, Kashmiri, Konkani, Maithili, Malayalam, Manipuri, Marathi, Nepali, Oriya, Punjabi, Sanskrit, Santhali, Sindhi, Tamil, Telugu, Urdu and English.

C. Interview

1. The candidate's interview will be conducted by an Interview Board, who will review his introduction. Most of the questions asked will be of a general nature. The intent of the capable and impartial observer's board is to assess whether the candidate has the right personality to assume the responsibilities of the Civil Services. The candidate's mental skills are also tested. Broadly they test not only the candidate's intelligence but also his aptitude and interest in social matters. A candidate can be tested for his mental alertness, ability to handle criticism, clarity of thoughts, ability to logically discuss, ability to take balance decisions, breadth and depth of interests, ability to lead and organise, commitment and integrity.

2. There is no cross-examination of candidates. A simple, amiable atmosphere is created to conduct the Interview in a particular direction and the conversation is set to a pattern in order to determine a candidate's mental skills.
3. The Interview does not intend to gauge a candidate's specialised knowledge or general knowledge as the same is already covered in the written tests. It is expected that a candidate should not just know the subjects he has studied but he must also be aware about and be sensitive to what is happening around him, both on the national and international fronts. He should also be aware of the latest developments and discoveries and whether they generate curiosity in him.

Note: For more detailed information on UPSC examinations, syllabus and pattern, please visit the website: www.upsc.gov.in.

❑

Preparing for the Examination

"Leaders are born in the moments of defeat. So, success is, in fact, embedded in successive defeats."

—Maharishi Aurobindo

The Civil Services examination is one of the most prestigious examinations of the country which evokes perpetual curiosity in the candidates. Nowadays, the youth are quite concerned about their job and career. Today every youth of the society desires a good job, so that he and his family can have a prosperous life. They, therefore, toil very hard to make the Civil Services their career.

The Civil Services are as popular today as they were during the British Raj. As we all know, the Civil Services are the backbone of the Indian administrative system. In our country, policy-making and its implementation is mainly the responsibility of the Civil Servants. That is the reason that they enjoy such awesome respect in the society.

Step-by-step Preparation

Thousands of aspirants take the UPSC examinations every year, but only a few hundred are selected. Though the examinations are very tough, an integrated approach with meticulous planning can help one achieve his aim.

Needless to say, several thousands of aspirants work very hard to prepare for the examinations. Some make it through the Preliminary, others through the Main, but very few make it to the Interview—many more are left disappointed.

Only 15,000–20,000 out of approximately four lakh candidates who appear for the preliminary examination get through this first step. Out of these, most of the candidates are eliminated in the main examination. The number of students called for the Interview is almost thrice the number of vacancies. For instance, if the number of vacancies is 1,000, the number of candidates who get the call letter for the Interview is approximately 3,000. Only a few get through to become an IFS, IAS or IPS officers. Others are selected for Indian Revenue Service (IRS) and other allied services.

The pattern of the examinations was changed to help students free themselves from the clutches of coaching classes who were fleecing them in the name of ensuring 'success'. However, the so-called coaching classes sprang back in less than a year's time. They are now offering courses for CSAT examination as well. Experts are of the view that the pattern of the examinations has become such that if one prepares for the post of a Collector, then he can appear for the Inspector's examination also. In other words, the new pattern has proved to be beneficial in taking other examinations, like the banking service and public service commission as well. So, separate preparations are not required for other examinations.

Prepare As Per the Pyramid

Whatever the examination, it is necessary to prepare a pyramid. Initially, we should start by covering the syllabus, but as the dates of the examinations come closer, we should follow the pattern set in the pyramid, that is, move down the pyramid.

Syllabus
Solved Question Bank
NCERT and Basic Books
Other Standard Books

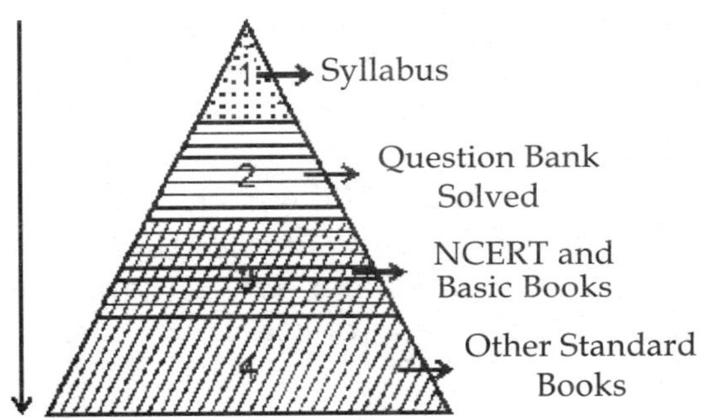

Formulate a Strategy

Formulating a strategy is essential for any examination. All successful candidates agree that preparations must be done according to one's own ability. While preparing your strategy, you need to assess how many days would be required to complete your preparations. Between different papers, there may be some gaps; these can also be used for the preparation. Time is all-important and if you make best use of it, you can maximize your chances of success. Devote more time on subjects which will get you a place on the merit list, but do not altogether ignore the qualifying subjects.

Every Moment is Important

Successful candidates are of the view that one stands a good chance to get through if he/she makes maximum use of the time leftover. During this time, do not study any new topics but revise thoroughly what you have already read. Revision is the key to success. Also, make a list of subjects on which questions are based and prepare accordingly. If you think that you lack preparedness in the GS paper and you can complete it in 2 days, you must deal with it first. Only then you must think of preparing for the other papers. You will have to formulate such plans yourself and also implement them yourself. This will help you make the best use of your spare time.

The questions asked are of Matriculation level. So, go through an English newspaper and study English-Hindi grammar every day.

Prepare Keeping the Gap Between Subjects in Mind

Successful people do not do anything different. They merely do things differently. So, you have to think of doing things differently to stand out from the crowd. First, take note of the dates of the optional papers. Usually, there is considerable gap between them. So, it would be wise to keep the preparations for such subjects for the intervening time and concentrate on revising those in which you are weak. This way you can buy some extra time to prepare for other subjects.

Concentrate on Compulsory Subjects

Candidates preparing for IAS Examination are usually not serious about General English and Hindi. As a result, they have to face a lot of hurdles later and sometimes end up blaming their poor planning and fate. The UPSC lays equal stress on every subject. You cannot afford to ignore any subject and move ahead. Only if you succeed in getting qualifying marks in these subjects, you will be evaluated further. So, do not make the mistake of ignoring the General English and Hindi papers.

As it has been pointed out earlier, the questions asked in these are of the Matriculation level. So, make sure to read an English newspaper and English-Hindi grammar every day.

Need for a Scientific Approach

Some of the toppers of the Main examinations say that some candidates think only a little preparation is required to do well in the Essay section. This view is a fallacy. You can only get good marks in the essay section, if you prepare scientifically.

It is better to identify an area of your interest and make up your mind to answer questions related to that area. For instance, if you decide that your essay topic would be politics, then you would be in a better situation and you can also complete your preparation.

Essay writing is compulsory and three hours are allotted to write an essay on a subject. You must write it thoughtfully, organise and rationalise it.

Make it a point to study 'Yojna' and 'Kurukshetra' magazines every month. Study the question papers of the previous years. It would be advisable to select two areas of interest and prepare them.

In this examination, there is a compulsory Essay Paper in which out of 4 subjects each given in two—A and B parts, after choosing any one subject from a part each, two Essays are required to be written, each of which should contain 1000–1200 words. You need to write the essay in a deliberately systemic and logical manner.

If we look at the subjects of the Essay Paper these days, they are mostly on philosophy, adage and proverb or on the sayings of a noble man.

Read the magazines 'Yojna', 'Kurukshetra' every month. See question papers of the last few years. Prepare for writing essays on two subjects of your interest chosen by you.

Practice is Essential

Essay writing tests your thinking process, language style and clarity of presentation. Practise writing essays. Moreover, if you know someone who has succeeded in the Civil Services Examinations, take his help to plan your preparations.

Improve Writing Skills

A common problem with IAS examination aspirants is that though they study very hard, they face difficulties in subjects like essay writing due to lack of writing practice. So, experts advise that you practise writing as much as possible as this will help you balance your thoughts and improve your writing speed. It is also believed that Essay writing is an uninterrupted activity where your style, command over language, views and knowledge of the topic are all put to test. So, in order to strike a balance among all of these attributes, it is essential to practise as much as possible.

Select Core Area in Every Subject

The best way to equip yourself in the minimum possible time is through the notes you have prepared. Experts suggest that instead of pouring yourself into voluminous books, it is better to go through the notes you have prepared throughout the year.

Remember, howsoever hard you might have studied, in preparing for a comprehensive examination like the Civil Services, you are bound to miss out something or the other. So, it is advisable to keep some back-up time to prepare for what you have missed out.

Keep a Tab on Word Limit

Confine yourself to the instructed word limit. Some candidates do not confine to the word limit. Consequently, they tend to overwrite, waste time and miss out on other questions which they could have answered.

The answer sought after must be written in the given number of words only and to the point. Some of the students do not comply with this guidance; they may face the problem that they may not be able to write answers for some of the questions, due to the time-lapse, even if they know the answers. The questions for the main examination these days are of 150 words and 250 words, for which 10 and 15 marks respectively are given. The total number of questions is 20. The General Studies paper of the main examination, Question Paper-IV, contains a total (including the case studies) of 12 questions.

Prepare from Question Papers of Previous Years

Based on your judgement, select questions of the optional subjects from the question papers of the past years and prepare their model answers. The questions usually have affiliated questions also and so keep in mind all possible aspects of the selected questions.

Maintain a Balance in Writing

Please remember that every word written by you in the IAS examination reflects your thought process and personality. Supporting explicitly any particular policy or party can be damaging for you. So, present a balanced view and use every word judiciously.

Revision is Necessary

The candidates must revise the different subjects in order of their preference. You also must practise writing the essay. In case you are facing difficulties in presenting the subject in a proper sequence, originality or anything related to the topic, then set it right while you still have time. The syllabus of the first question paper of General Studies is stereotyped, just keep this in mind and prepare yourself.

Time Management is Important

If you want to ensure success in the Main Examination, pay equal attention to all the question papers. Paying extra attention to some papers and ignoring others does not help.

To brighten your chances for selection, it is essential to secure maximum marks in all the papers. It entirely depends on you to get as close as possible to the total 1,750 marks. Getting more marks will not only ensure selection but also improve your ranking, so that you can get a position as an IAS, IFS or any other cadre official.

Keeping an eye on time is important while preparing for the examination. Devote equal time to all the subjects. Each question also must be given equal time, else in dealing with the questions of your interest, you will miss out on others. Moreover, the questions you know you can answer better than others must be dealt with first. You must also note that you may devote about 35 minutes to each of the optional questions. While answering the question paper on General Studies, accuracy is important. In addition to accuracy, you also need to maintain your speed.

Some Important Tips

- Study the syllabus in depth and thoroughly analyse the question papers of the past 10 years. Give ample time to both as it will facilitate you to devise your preparation strategy.
- The syllabus is divided into sections and sub-sections. With the help of questions collection or trend analysis (if available), try to determine from which section or sub-section questions are being generally framed and the likelihood in the future.
- It is not enough to have knowledge of the fundamentals in the Preliminary Examination. All perceptions, conceptions, practical applications, future possibilities and interrelationships associated with the fundamentals must also be learned.
- Now, according to the sections and sub-sections of the syllabus, it is time to prepare concise, precise and exam-related notes. First, write the name of the section in bold letters. Then, write the name of the first sub-section as the title. Now, write everything related to the topic in a bullet form. Now, the question arises on what to write and what to leave out. The key to this question lies in careful study and analysis of the syllabus and question

bank, study the trend, understand the demands of the examination, avoid being confused by too many facts and data and simplify the complicated data.

- Judiciously make brief notes, but not so brief that you do not understand the context while revising.
- Freely use pictures, diagrams, tables, underlining, signs and different coloured pens while preparing the notes. Wherever there is possibility of change of facts and data, use a pencil, so that they can be altered by erasing. This will help you keep your notebook neat.
- Leave some blank space after every sub-section so that if required, you may add additional matter.
- For making notes, buy a fine-looking diary (as expensive as you can afford it). Maintain it properly so that you retain your interest in it.
- Being a scholar in a subject and passing it are two separate things. So, while preparing the notes, you need not cover all the important facts, rather cover those facts which you feel are important, keeping in mind the question bank and trend analysis.
- After preparing the topicwise notes prepare a few lists in the diary related to optional subject(s), like book, writer, person and assigned completion time related to the optional subject(s). While concluding, if you feel, make further notes.
- While preparing the notes, keep the question bank and trend analysis handy. Before you start making notes on any topic, analyse in detail all the questions which have been set.
- Prepare and use appropriate markings for indicating what is most important, important, less important et cetera.
- The topic(s) on which more questions have been set in the past, analyse and study them thoroughly.
- Revise questions from the question bank in examination hall-type settings. After you have mastered them, then revise the standard practice set.
- Keep revising your notes and keep noting all points which will help you in the examination.
- Discuss different topics with your upto-the-mark friends.

- Form an upto-the-mark friends' group and revise together.
- Think and review each topic from different angles and aspects.
- Do not stay away from your syllabus and question bank. Distancing yourself from them means you are distancing yourself from success.
- After preparing your notes, learn them and try to recall them.
- Normally, the preliminary examination is held in the third week of May. So, you must complete your notes' preparation latest by 15th February.
- After preparing notes on a topic, practise answering as many related questions as possible.
- Select a topic for making notes. Gather all material available on the topic, that is, books, coaching material etc. Study thoroughly only that topic from all the available material, highlight the important facts, then after understanding fully make notes in your own handwriting.
- From 15th February to 31st March, try to memorise word by word as many notes as possible.
- From 1st April to the examination date (approximately 50 days), practise answering questions from the question bank and practise set regularly. Revise and memorise the notes.
- Maintain the study material in good condition.
- Study as much material as possible till you start making the notes, but after making the notes, study only the notes or basic book repeatedly.
- It is better to study one book ten times rather than study ten books once.
- Even in the free time (while eating or before sleeping), keep thinking about the highlights of the notes. Try to frame new questions related to a topic and discuss them.

HUMAN INSIGHT – 1

How do we learn and remember?

83% Seeing
11% Hearing
3.5% Smelling
1.5% Touching
1% Tasting

HUMAN INSIGHT – 2

How do we retain information?

10% What we read
20% What we hear
30% What we see
50% What we see and hear
70% What we say
90% What we say and perform

HUMAN INSIGHT – 3

ACTION	RECALL AFTER 3 HOURS	RECALL AFTER 3 DAYS
Spoken while alone	70%	10%
Shown while alone	72%	20%
Spoken and shown while alone	85%	65%

SOME USEFUL HINTS

Take care of yourself
Take care of your family
Put up a calendar in front of your study-table
Organise yourself
Draw a priority list
Time management
Stay away from bad company and do not stray
Treat every new subject seriously
Develop a hobby
Take care of your funds and spend wisely
Do not be overambitious
Speak less, listen more and reflect most.

SEVEN HABITS OF MOST INFLUENTIAL PERSONS

Take initiative
Visualise the end result before commencing anything
Follow the priority list
Always think of succeeding
Make efforts to understand first

Work as a team (in this case, form a study group)

Sharpen your skills by taking memory tonics and effective time management.

TEN TIPS FOR PREPARATION

Fix your aim
Plan properly
Start early
Keep serious approach
Maintain punctuality
Identify your weak points
Choose quality material
Keep honest approach
Frequently test yourself
Consult your teachers and wise friends.

❑

Formula for Getting Better Marks

Every good work appears impossible initially.

—Thiruvalluvar

For the main examination apart, from hard work, the selection of a high-scoring subject is also important. For this reason, some subjects are considered hot in the main examination. A large number of candidates are selecting philosophy as the second option, apart from other subjects. According to experts philosophy is not only a high-scoring subject, but its syllabus is also limited as compared to other subjects. If you are interested in philosophy and you have opted for it as the main subject, then you can secure top marks in it.

STUDY OF PHILOSOPHY SYLLABUS

For the main examination, the syllabus of philosophy has been divided in three parts—history of philosophy and its problems, its socio-political aspects and its religious aspects. Two question papers are framed from these three parts for the main examination. So, on the basis of the nature of the question paper, it can be divided into sub-sections. As part of the history of philosophy and its problems, western and Indian philosophies have been included. Again, to make it easier for the study of western philosophy, it has been divided into traditional western philosophy (related to the logic and perception school of thought) and contemporary western philosophy (related to language analytics). This way western philosophy and Indian philosophy comprise the first question paper, while the second paper comprises social, political and religious philosophies.

Prepare According to the Syllabus

In the first question paper of Philosophy, a total of 11 philosophies and their chosen principles are part of the syllabus. The first five among the 11 are traditional western philosophies and the next six are language-based analytical philosophies. In the section on Indian philosophy, a total of 9 philosophies and their selected principles have been included. The second question paper comprises of social-political philosophy and religious philosophy and 10 topics from both have been included in the syllabus.

Keep Yourself Updated

The syllabus of Philosophy underwent a major change in 2008. Earlier, in traditional western philosophy, some chosen philosophers and their selected philosophical principles were studied, but now philosophers and their principles have been included according to schools of thought. In contemporary western philosophy, the principles of Wittgenstein and Heidegger have been included in the syllabus. As for contemporary Indian philosophy, Sri Aurobindo's principles of evolution and 'purna yoga' (integral yoga) have been included. In social-political philosophies, some topics have also been changed. Normally, religious philosophy is not a part of CSAT.

It is through CSAT that candidates of all the subjects have been brought on the same level. This has ended the practice of memorising and the focus has now shifted to logical reasoning, understanding, individuality and interpretation. Now, an examinee's thoughts, command over language, decision-making ability and swiftness in interpreting and calculating are put to test.

CSAT has been divided into different categories. Each category has some tactics. Some of the tactics are given below:

Hindi/English Language

The first part of CSAT will have portions in Hindi and English. Questions will be asked on the basis of given prose. The prose must be read carefully before answering the questions based on it. The examinee should answer the questions in the language he had opted for in his application form. If Hindi has been opted then read the Hindi prose and answer it in Hindi.

Mathematics

In CSAT, your accuracy will be judged by mathematics. The syllabus will be based on NCERT (6–10) mathematics text book up to class 10. There will be question on percentage, average, age, time and work, time and distance and probability, etc. By repeated practice, you can make this section easy to handle in a short time. Remember some of the basics, like squares of 1-50, square roots of 1-10, and so on. It is important to concentrate while solving this portion.

Decision-making

Taking decisions is the main function of an administrator. A right decision can permanently settle a problem. While taking any decision, it is important to analyse all the information and figures related to the problem. This tells a lot about an examinee's understanding, knowledge, patience and initiative capability. So, such questions must be divided into phases and then solved. This tests an ordinary person's or administrator's decision-making capability, nimbleness, etc. He must keep humanity, constitution and legislation in mind before taking a decision. For instance, if you get the information that a bomb has been planted in a mall, do not panic. Inform the mall manager and have the place vacated calmly.

Ability to Communicate

A public servant has to communicate with the general public, politicians, media and employees. So, every public servant must have the ability to contact/communicate/speak with different people at different places and time. An administrator must give information based on facts. No information given by him must hurt or violate the constitution, court, assembly or the general public. The communication must be direct, simple and brief. It must be kept in mind that all contacts are established through official agencies or channels.

Ability to Reason

The mental abilities of an examinee are put to test. Most of the questions will be in the form of a puzzle which they have to solve. The book by RS Aggarwal is quite helpful. The book has many questions in the form of puzzles. With regular practice, the questions can be solved in much less time.

Mental Capability

In a manner, it tests your logical capability. In this, an event has to be proved on the basis of certain statistics or data. Here again, RS Aggarwal's book is very helpful.

Test of English and Comprehension

This section will be only in English for all the candidates. Questions are asked based on a given prose. Read the prose carefully before answering the questions. This section has some questions on grammar also and any book of class X level will be helpful. Revise and practise for this section from the question papers of UPSC's multi-purpose English examinations of the previous years, as many times as possible. This will help you understand the pattern and will also help you in the examination.

CSAT is a blessing for students who believe in understanding the subject matter rather than plain memorising. A time will come when there will be more public servants with logical ability.

Points to Remember

Maintain a fixed number of hours for study every day. Instead of studying for 14 hours on one day and then for 2 hours the next, it is better to study for 10 hours every day.

Study in groups. This will help you clear your doubts and you will also enjoy it. Fix a target for each day and try to achieve it.

In order to acquire command over language, you must follow the five golden rules of reading, writing, listening, speaking and arguing logically.

The Civil Services cover a vast area of work and in diverse fields. So, study all issues related to general events in depth.

To understand the fundamentals of a subject, study NCERT books and keep your target in mind.

During spare time, read inspiring books like 'Time Management' and 'You Can Win.'

Useful Exam-related Material

A brief list of newspapers and magazines that can be useful in preparing for the Civil Services Examination:

Dainik Jagran, Hindustan, Dainik Bhaskar, Economic Times, Pratiyogita Darpan, Chanakya, Civil Services Today, Civil Services Chronicle, Civil Services Times, Arihant, Samsamyiki Mahasagar, Panorama Samasamyiki, Vigyan Pragati, Science Reporter, Yojna, Kurukshetra, Aha Zindagi, India Today, Outlook, Manorama Year Book, Bharat (Year Book) and Unique General Knowledge.

Watch and Listen to:

DD News, DD Bharti, Lok Sabha TV News, Rajya Sabha TV news, BBC London Radio.

Important Websites

upsc.giv.in, pib.gov.in, moef.gov.in, dst.gov.in, meity.gov.in, india.gov.in/topics/art-culture

History

Ancient India (Old NCERT) – Ram Sharan Sharma (Class XI)
Medieval India (Old NCERT) – Satish Chandra (Class XI)
Modern India (Old NCERT) – Bipin Chandra (Class XII)
History of Modern India (Spectrum) – Rajiv Ahir
Struggle for Independence – Bipin Chandra
Indian Art and Culture – Nitin Singhania

Geography

Oxford Student Atlas
Geography (Old NCERT) – Class VI to Class IX
Theory of Human Geography (New NCERT) – Class XI
India, People and Economy (New NCERT) – Class XII

Physical Environment of India (NCERT) – Class XII
Geography of India (Periyar Publication) – Arvind Kumar.

Indian Polity and Constitution

Social and Political Life (New NCERT) – Class VI to VII
Democratic and Political Life (New NCERT) – Class IX & X
Constitution of India, Theory and Behaviour (New NCERT) – Class XI
Indian Polity – M. Laxmikant
Our Constitution – Subhash Kashyap or D.D. Basu
Constitution of India (Periyar Publication) – Arvind Kumar and Avinash Shekhar

Economics and Indian Economy

Understanding of Economic Development (New NCERT) – Class XI
Indian Economy – An Introduction (Unique Publication) – Sanjiv Verma

General Science and Science and Technology

Science (New NCERT) – Class IX and X
Biology (New NCERT) – Class XII
Special issue of General Science (Pratiyogita Darpan)
Vigyan Pragati
Science and Technology – Ravi Agrahari
Update General Awareness based on news papers

Internal Security

Internal Security of India and its Main Challanges – Ashok Kumar

Ethics Integrity and Aptitude

Chronicle Publication

CSAT

Arithmetic – R.S. Aggarwal
Logical Reasoning – R.S. Aggarwal
Quantitative Aptitude – R.S. Aggarwal
CSAT Ptactice Set – Madhukar Kotwe

Political Science

Outline of Political Thought – O.P. Gaba
International Politics – B.S. Phadia
International Relation in 21st Century – Pushpesh Pant.
Constitution of India: An Introduction – D.D. Basu
Our Constitution – Subhash Kashyap
Our Parliament – Subhash Kashyap
Our Political System – Subhash Kashyap
Political Science (NCERT) – Class X and XI

❑

6

Always Keep Your Mind Active

People who read a lot but do not use their brain, are unable to think.

—Albert Einstein

Like the body, the mind also needs to be well-organised in order to remain healthy. A few tips are being offered which will not only make your mind work faster, but will help you remember things without difficulty while preparing for the examination.

Prepare yourself to exercise your brain. It is different from physical exercise. Chess was invented in India. It is the most rigorous and effective mental exercise. Anyway, chess is not played by everyone, but almost everyone enjoys solving the crossword puzzle or playing solitaire on the computer. You may start with them. Sudoku is also quite effective. If they do not appeal to you, you may try simple addition-subtraction and multiplication-division.

Try to learn a joke or a poem once a week. This will keep your mind in shape and increase its retention capacity. Try to do something new every time and let your mind be engaged with new ideas. Thinking like a child will also do. Children think positively, have amazing ideas and lots of curiosity.

Do not stop yourself from daydreaming. This will sharpen your mind and heighten its power. Try to develop multifaceted personalities and think in as many different ways as possible.

Expel the Examination Fever

Some examinees become nervous at the very thought of appearing for the examination. Lot of questions unnerve them—"Will I be able to answer all the questions?" and "It would have been better had I studied a little more." A little pressure, though, is good for the examinees as it produces adrenaline, a hormone which keeps us alert and helps us to concentrate.

It is natural to feel some stress and pressure, but too much anxiety can be disturbing. It engulfs the person in negative thoughts and he is unable to focus or concentrate. This affects the performance level of a candidate as he is neither able to concentrate on the questions, nor able to answer them correctly. There are quite a few ways by which a candidate can expel the examination fever and give his best during the examination.

Prior to an Examination

Complete the syllabus well ahead of time and complete the revision work at least a day prior to the examination. Tension mounts if one keeps studying till the last moment. To keep the mind cool and steady, one can adopt various means—some feel relaxed listening to music, some by exercising, even taking bath in lukewarm water can be a good idea. Any of these relaxing means can be tried.

Such means can be very helpful if applied on the day of the examination and a day before it. It helps you remember what you have read and boosts your confidence. Even not knowing the route to the examination centre can be a cause for worry. Try to be certain about the exact location of the examination venue and visit it once before the day of the examination. This will help you remain calm. Read the examination instructions carefully. Have a sound sleep on the eve of the examination.

During the Examinations

"I know nothing." If you have not studied well, this feeling is bound to bother you. However, despite studying well, if you have such feelings, it is an indication of tension. Stress prevents you from concentrating. Some candidates are even unable to read the questions properly. Some ways to ease the stress are given below:

- Reach the examination hall well in time.
- Once you reach the examination hall, take a few deep breaths. Usually candidates have irregular breathing due to tension. Keep your backbone straight while taking deep breaths.
- Look at some stationary lifeless object like the wall or a picture in front of you and try to concentrate.
- Repeat some positive thoughts like 'I am going to pass this examination.' Keep repeating this thought for a minute or two. It will relax you.
- Recall your achievements. It will boost your confidence.
- Read the questions carefully. If you tend to feel nervous during the course of the examination, repeat the concentration technique.
- Quickly prepare a strategy to answer the question paper, like the order of answering the questions, etc. and, without wasting time, start answering the questions.

Ways to Enhance Your Memory

In order to remember something, the brain decides on an issue's meaning, use and justification. The brain's priority follows the same order. The first step to memory is to know the meaning; therefore, to remember anything, is necessary to know its meaning. If the meaning is not understood, then there is no point in mugging it. So, to remember anything or any course material, first understand its meaning, then its importance and usefulness and, finally, its justification.

❑

7

Devise Your Own Strategy

Adhishthanam tatha karta karan ch prathgivadham.
Vividhasch prathakcheshta daiv chaivatra panchmam

—Srimad Bhagvadgita

To achieve success in any task, five things are essential. *Aadhisthan* (determination), *karta* (the doer), *karan* (means), *cheshta* (effort) and *daiv* (fate, the Almighty's blessings).

To succeed in the civil services examination, your strategy is most important. This is the one examination in which you cannot be successful through anyone else's support. It is your self-confidence, your willpower and your inspiration that will help you achieve success. If you have a very powerful inspiration to succeed, then it is definitely bound to help. The inspiration could be social service, desire to make a name in the society or the desire to win over the person you love.

Take a notebook and jot down all the details which you can get from newspapers/magazines or by talking to persons who have succeeded. The information must be relevant.

Choose your optional subject with due consideration, keeping in mind your interest, availability of study material, type of questions and scoring, etc. Take as many suggestions as possible, but follow your gut feeling. Understand that the subject is not important; it is your grasp on the subject and your success that matters.

For the Preliminary and Main examinations, prepare a strategy for every aspect. Analyse your strengths and weaknesses. Prepare a strategy which builds on your strengths, minimises your weaknesses and try to convert them into strengths.

Prepare essays from the very beginning. You can prepare essays on many topics of General Studies, which relate to social issues.

While preparing yourself, your entire focus should be on the Main examination. To prepare for the Preliminary examination, six months are sufficient. You can change your strategy according to your needs, but do remember that even before the Preliminary examination, you have started preparing for the Main examination. This will give you necessary self-confidence.

Choice of Optional Subjects

Some subjects can be opted on account of being high scoring, require normal preparation and lots of essay topics are from these subjects. These subjects are—Geography, Political Science, Public Administration, History and Sociology, which are simpler and can be prepared with normal studies. Particularly, there are 30-35 questions from Geography in the Preliminary examination. Whereas, in the Main examinations, questions of 120 marks are asked each from Geography, History and Political Science. The topics in the Essay-writing section are mostly related to Sociology, Geography, History and Economics.

Selecting the Medium

There is no discrimination on account of the medium of language opted in the Civil Services examination. Though you can qualify both in Hindi and English medium, students succeed more in English medium. The reason is the lack of availability of adequate study material in Hindi and whatever is available lacks authenticity and depth. The questions and model answers are based on standard English books. So, students, who opt for Hindi medium, must go through the English books also.

Importance of Science

The selection of Science as a subject is gradually diminishing in the Civil Services examinations. The reason is the vastness of the subject and its complexities. Students of Science should choose subjects which are based on the fundamental principles of Science, but the subject-matter is associated with our daily life like Geography, which combines Science and Art?

Preparing for the Interview

It is a misconception that a candidate's knowledge is tested during the interview. Actually, it is an assessment of his/her personality traits, suitability and aptitude and both moral and ethical beliefs. It is a test of his/her psychology, sensitiveness to what is happening around him/her and the capacity to take decisions according to the demands of the situation. Do not be narrow-minded and confine yourself to regional views but present opinions relevant to the national level.

Some Important Tips

General Studies (Preliminary Examination):

- Read all the NCERT books (old and new) of classes 5–12 thoroughly. These are most important. So, even if they consume extra time, do not worry.
- Make concise notes in a diary.
- While studying Geography, keep an Atlas in front of you.
- Practise from the question bank.
- Read newspapers everyday. Listen to the news on TV.
- Discuss current affairs with your friends.
- Read magazines like *Pratiyogita Darpan, Science Reporter, Chronicle, Yojna, Frontline* and *India Today*, among others, regularly.
- You must read the *Pratiyogita Darpan* supplement '*Bharatiya Arthvyavastha*' (Indian Economy).
- *Bharatiya Rajyavyavastha* by D.D. Basu, Subhash Kashyap BARE ACT, NCERT.
- *Bharatiya Itihaas*—Unique Guide, Kiran Prakashan, NCERT.
- *Bharat Sandarbh Granth*—Chronicle or Manorama Year Book.

- Read the Unique Guide thoroughly so that all the topics are covered. Underline the important points.
- Solve question bank and practise sets before the examinations.
- Go through the trend analysis.
- Prepare a synopsis of all the NCERT books and revise them again and again.
- In the diary with notes, draw diagrams, pictures, paste paper cuttings and use multi-coloured symbols to mark important points.
- If you feel it necessary, take part in a Test Series of a local coaching centre.
- Study, prepare notes and collect study material till April 15. Then, for the last 30 days (prior to the examination), solve practice sets, test sets and question banks everyday. It helps you a lot if you do this in a group.
- Make use of 'memory tricks'. Read some books on memory power enhancement.
- Use TTK or Oxford Atlas. Try to photo memorise the Atlas.
- A month or so before the examinations, go through the magazines related to contemporary affairs like 'Youth', 'Vikas' and 'Pratiyogita Darpan'.
- Since there is negative marking, desist from the tendency to read up everything on every section or topic. Instead, the better option is to study one book on each section or topic thoroughly and try to remember all that you have read. Study the sections/topics of your interest thoroughly so that you do not miss out on any question in them. Study the other sections/topics normally.
- Two days before the examinations, buy all important items like 2-3 pencils, eraser, cutter, 2 pens, among other things.
- Fifteen days before the examinations, stop looking at new books on the traditional part of GS (History, Geography and Political Science). Revise only whatever you have read till now and solve practice sets.

- Fifteen days prior to the examinations, focus on current affairs. Revise only the Atlas, GS, notes, synopsis and selected books and the highlighted parts.
- Stop studying a day before the examinations, enjoy yourself and stay cool. I used to go out for a shave at the salon, and then visit a friend's house, where I listened to the ghazals of Jagjit Singh and Ghulam Ali over a cup of tea. I would return to my room by 9 pm, have my dinner and sleep. I would get up at 5 am the next morning, the day of the examination.
- On the day of the examination, get up early, go through your daily grind, have a bath and then after a light breakfast, proceed to the examination centre with a positive feeling. Think that you have put in a lot of hard work and have done your best and so the outcome will be positive. Use your own vehicle or reserve a vehicle to take you to the examination centre. On the way to the examination centre, recall all the achievements of which you are proud and remember your parents, elders, friends, relatives and the Almighty. Remember that their blessings and good wishes are with you, and so you will definitely be selected. Be as cheerful as possible.
- Keep drinking cold water/juice. Keep remembering whoever you worship or are inspired by. Be happy and positive.
- After reaching the examination centre, look for your roll number, room number and other details. Never sit in a crowd, so that their conversation does not disturb your calm frame of mind. Try to sit at a cool/clean place from where the main gate of the examination hall and other candidates are visible and it is relatively quieter. Stay calm and repeat what you had done while coming to the centre. Keep your mind calm, be confident and remain cheerful.
- If you are going to take the examinations with a friend, never talk anything about the examinations with him on way or on reaching the examination centre. Keep

doing what has been suggested above. If you need to talk to him, share a joke or two and laugh it out or do anything which will relax you.

- If you need to use the washroom, do so. Else, settle down quietly at your seat and keep a bottle of water and a handkerchief beside you. Do not look at the other candidates or their actions. This time close your eyes and repeat what has been suggested above.
- When you get your question paper and are instructed to open it, do so, concentrate and start from your strength. Be patient and understand the question, do not rush as you might misinterpret and make an error of judgement.
- Maintain a steady pace while answering the questions, neither too slowly nor too fast.
- During the lunch break, have something light and digestible, along with some juice.
- After the Preliminary examination, do not waste time in thinking of its outcome. Start preparations for the Main examination.
- There is usually a gap of five months between the Preliminary and the Main examinations. So, start preparing for the Main examinations without wasting any time.
- Go through the question bank and trend analysis. Be selective in preparing a few guess questions. You can take help from the guess papers and trend analysis available in the market.
- While making notes for the Main examinations, do not use a diary. Use A4 size papers. Leave ¼ margin on both sides as is the case in the answer sheets given for the Main examinations.
- According to your guess, prioritise the topics and write them down at one place. Then start making the topic-wise notes on a priority basis. Before making notes on a particular topic, look up the related questions in the question bank. Then read all material available related to the topic. Decide on the important points, which will

form parts of the answer and then jot them down in bullets form.

- Follow all the instructions given on the last page of the answer sheet of the Main examinations to the last letter. There are important instructions to be followed, like writing PTO, drawing a line after completing every answer, writing the question number and page number on the first page and not making any marks or symbols on the answer sheet.
- Stick to the word limit compulsorily.
- Wherever possible, write the comparisons and inter-connections.
- Use your own language as far as possible that is easy and simple. It should not be very common or very sophisticated.
- The conclusion must always be impartial and positive.
- First, understand the demands/intent of the question, then mentally frame the answer and then start answering.
- Your answers must be unique and different from others. It is suggested that you learn only the important facts and data from books and other study material. To improve your language, read some literature, read the editorials in newspapers, in short, anyhow considering the circumstances make it suitable, simple, clear and sensitive. You will always get the benefit of this, even during the Interview.
- Avoid giving unnecessary and out-of-context arguments.
- The introduction should not be of more than 2-3 lines. In questions that ask for opinion, it is not necessary to give introduction or conclusion.
- Keep the answer-sheet well organised. Your handwriting must be good. Follow all the instructions carefully. All this can help you get good marks.
- In optional subjects, memorise some important words and sentences which can create a good impact. Use them in your answers as much as possible.
- Avoid errors in spellings, grammar and sentence construction. To identify such mistakes, you may show

your answers to a senior or a teacher and have them corrected. You can also take dictation tests from time to time.

- Your handwriting should be clear and neat as it helps in getting additional marks. For this, practise writing as much as possible. Keep appropriate space between words. Change paragraphs.
- Stick to the demands of the question and write only what is asked for. Writing to display your intelligence can be damaging.
- While preparing, if you are not satisfied with your answers, take the help of a teacher/senior.
- Do not overwrite or cut or delete words. Develop the habit of thinking first and then writing.
- You may use English words while answering, but in Devanagari font.
- Do not use too many quotes of scholars. Use your own language as much as possible.
- Every optional subject has a distinctive vocabulary and language. Make sure you present the same vocabulary and language.
- Underline important words, facts, statistics, sentences and names.
- If you are writing with a black pen, underline with a blue pen and if you are using a blue pen, underline with a black pen.
- Start a new answer on a fresh page.
- After every question paper, start preparing for the next paper with full attention.
- Do not worry or reflect over the past question papers. It does no good, only harm.
- Always give a head rule above the words, if writing in Hindi.

Twenty-five Inspiring Thoughts

1. Winners don't do different things, they do things differently.

—Shiv Khera

2. If you fool me once, shame on you. If you fool me twice, shame on me.
3. Freedom without discipline leads to destruction.
4. Study as if you will live forever. Live as if you will die tomorrow.

—Mahatma Gandhi

5. It is much better to deserve an honour and not get it, rather than not deserve it and yet get it.

—Mark Twain

6. A smooth sea never made a skilful mariner.
7. Suicide is a permanent solution for a temporary problem.
8. The critic is one who knows the price of everything and the value of nothing.

—Oscar Wilde

9. Trifles make perfection and perfection is no trifle.

—Michelangelo

10. No risk, no gain.

—Ray Kroc (McDonald's Founder)

11. The easier way may actually be the tougher way.
12. Even a stopped watch gives the right time twice in a day.
13. Ways to create a good viewpoint: (i) Change focus, look for positivity, (ii) Make a habit of doing it now, (iii) Develop a conviction of gratitude, (iv) Get into a continuous educational programme.
14. Never leave for tomorrow what you can do today.

—Benjamin Franklin

15. When you are good to others, you are good to yourself.

— Benjamin Franklin

16. Stay away from bad company.
17. Learn to admire things that are necessary.
18. Bigger the hurdle, bigger the opportunity.
19. Trifles can make a big difference and to be big is no small matter.
20. Every opportunity comes but once in life.
21. Hurdles are such dreadful things which you notice only when you deviate from your aim.

22. The world does not appear the way it is, but the way we are.
23. We must keep an open mind, not an empty mind.
24. Always remember the 8 'Ps': Purpose, principle, planning, preparation, practice, perseverance, patience and pride.
25. Not taking any risk is in itself the biggest risk.

—Erica Jong

How to Win Friends and Influence People—25 Golden Rules

—By Dale Carnegie

1. Don't criticize, condemn or complain.
2. Give honest and sincere appreciation.
3. Become genuinely interested in other people.
4. Remember that a person's name is to that person the sweetest and most important sound in any language.
5. Be a good listener. Encourage others to talk about them.
6. Talk in terms of the other person's interests.
7. Make the other person feel important and do it sincerely.
8. The only way to get the best of an argument is to avoid it.
9. Show respect for the other person's opinion. Never say, "You are wrong."
10. If you are wrong, admit it quickly and emphatically.
11. Begin in a friendly way.
12. Get the other person saying 'Yes, Yes' immediately.
13. Let the other person do a great deal of the talking.
14. Try honestly to see things from the other person's point of view.
15. Be sympathetic to the other person's ideas and desires.
16. Talk about your own mistakes before criticizing the other person.
17. Ask questions instead of giving direct orders.
18. Let the other person save face.
19. Praise the slightest improvement and praise every improvement. Be hearty in your approbation and lavish in your praise.

20. Give the other person a fine reputation to live up to.
21. Use encouragement. Make the fault seem easy to correct.
22. Make the other person happy about doing the thing you suggest.
23. Let the other person feel that the idea is his or hers.
24. A true friend never gets in your way unless you happen to be going down.
25. Friendship is a single soul dwelling in two bodies.

Time Management

In any examination preparation, time management is essential. Preparing for nine papers in such a short time is not easy. This, however, can be made easy by time management. It can be done according to an individual's capability. For the Main examination, study at least for 10 hours. Since the general studies syllabus is quite extensive, allot 4 hours for it.

Practise Writing

It happens at times that despite knowing the answer to a question, you are unable to answer it properly. This could be because of two reasons, first you are not fast enough and second, lack of time management. This happens because you are unable to regulate your writing speed according to available time. To rectify this, select a self-framed question or a model question from a book and try to answer it in the allotted time without break. In the examination hall, you may not be able to complete all the questions due to paucity of time or not being able to stick to the word limit. Avoid being confused or going astray and answer the questions correctly.

Some Success Mantras

- To make your answers notable, use Writer's sayings and examples on related aspects of the question.
- Comprehensively study the important works of the leading writers and authors.
- Focus on brief notes and explanations.
- Remain stress-free by time management.

- Ensure that there are no grammatical errors in the Hindi paper.
- In the examination hall, for the questions which seem difficult use your knowledge maintaining your mental balance.
- While answering, to maintain continuity over your language, practise reading and writing.
- Take the help of an experienced guide for assessing your practice answer papers.
- Pay special attention to syllabus which has been added, after the change.
- In the essay to project unbiased view, maintain a balance between the 'for' and 'against' arguments.
- While following the contemporary events, pay special attention to its related aspects.
- Do not overlook the constitutional aspects of administrative tasks.
- To make your answers notable do mention the names of books written by scholars, their principles and recommendations. You can prepare a list of some of the scholars and their principles.
- While answering in the examination hall do your own appraisal, it should not be of the scholars or writers.
- Analyse the questions of the past years and try to identify the main topics and the trend of the questions.
- Draft answers to all the questions and practise accordingly.
- List authentic facts properly. Wrong facts create negative impression.
- Prepare specially for questions and short notes carrying two marks. You can score almost 100 per cent marks in them.
- While solving model questions, practise to answer them to the point.
- Raise the level of your writing style so that your answers reflect a civil servant's mentality and expansive thinking.
- While maintaining the flow of your language, if there are more than one dimensions implied in the questions,

try to connect them. Regularly read newspapers and magazines and make notes of the important facts.

- After carefully analysing the past year's questions, highlight the important portions or questions. This will help you prepare the complete syllabus.
- To be creative in your writing, pay special attention to understanding the fundamental theme of the topic. This will enhance your analytical ability also.
- Since the answers to the questions require detailed description, regular writing practice is most essential.
- Ensure that the answer is based on facts. Keep it as close to the main concepts and ideas, so that you do not go astray. Avoid being biased or prejudiced while answering because it can be quite damaging.
- While preparing, keep in mind the weightage of important subjects from the point of view of the examination.
- While answering keep track of the time, additional time taken to answer a question means you have less time for the other questions.
- In the main examinations, marks are not given for superficial answers. So, lay due importance on studying all the critical aspects.
- It is not enough to list the facts. Develop an analyst's point of view.
- Make brief notes of the likely and important chapters.
- Practise notes preparation as much as possible.
- Try to explain your concept in simplest language.
- In some subjects, maps-related questions are also asked. So prepare for them specially.
- Talk to experts on particular subjects. Cover as many past questions as possible. You will be able to answer the questions with clarity.

Success Tips

They are—devotion towards your objective, the willpower to work hard, the need to study at least for a year, proper selection of the optional subjects, study of the established books, grasp over contemporary events, good command over language, making short notes, reading basic books for learning theory, regular reading of newspapers and magazines, learning the past questions a must, continuous practise of the difficult questions, serious study of the IGNOU and NCERT books, preparation of notes, practising lots of answer writing, paying attention to time management, distributing your time equitably to all the questions, keeping track of the important national and international events, regular studying of the books and magazines published by the government.

Prepare as per the syllabus. Go through the past years' questions. Prepare geography scientifically. Study NCERT book to clarify the concepts. Reading is necessary to prepare for conceptual questions. Pay special attention to data, questions related to the atlas, economic survey and questions on census.

Use the atlas to prepare a list of physical landmarks, geographic structures, cities, etc. and study them. For geography, the more you work on the atlas, the better will be your scores. Instead of reading many books, read the selected and recognised books by reputed writers.

How to Make Notes

Notes are very important for preparation of the civil services examination. Good notes help you to prepare a balanced and inspiring strategy. They also help you to revise your syllabus in quick time. The method of making such notes is quite simple.

Linear Notes

This procedure is suitable for candidates who for the lack of time are unable to make detailed notes. Under this procedure, the study material itself is used and the important points and facts (date, statistics, etc.) are underlined using different coloured pens or pencils. But this procedure works only if the entire matter is systematically organised, otherwise you waste time in compiling the matter. It is better that you make notes on a plain register or loose sheets. Use only half page, so that you can add any facts or matter which you obtain later.

Pattern Notes

This procedure is also called the skeleton procedure. In this a subject is divided in different chapters and topics. Then the main points and facts of each topic are listed as headings or in pictorial form and all such mini-points are consolidated. It is easy to revise, as well as you save time too. You are able to understand the subject and topic relatively easily. Such notes act as a magic potion towards the end. You are able to understand the subject completely and formulate a clear strategy.

The undated data related to the Civil Service Examination, which have been taken mainly from the yearly reports of the Union Public Service Commission. In the data mentioned ahead for the candidates, how many candidates in total participated in the civil services examination, out of them, how many presented themselves for the preliminary examination, the main examination and the interview, and on the basis of the performance of the candidates, how many of them were finally selected, the information/data on this has been presented. Besides, the preliminary examination in the recent years, the main examination and the cut off of the final marks (according to the performance of the candidates under each category or class), the data thereof has been given.

In another table, an analysis of how many questions were asked in all the subjects of the general studies in the preliminary examination, the current trends in them, has been made.

Similarly, a detail of subject-wise analyses, which means how many questions and in which subject have been asked in the recent years, has been given in respect of all the four question papers relating to general study in the main examination. There is only one purpose behind giving all these data and that is—the candidate should prepare their strategy for the examination by looking at the trends.

No. of Applicants (2011–2019) UPSC Annual Report					
Year	No. of Applicants	No. of candidates appeared	No. of candidate qualified for mains exam	No. of candidates appeared in Personality Test	Final Selection
2011	499120	243236	11837	2415	999
2012	550080	271442	12795	2674	998
2013	776604	324279	14800	3001	1122
2014	947428	446623	16706	3308	1236
2015	945908	465882	15008	2797	1078
2016	1128262	459659	15382	2961	1099
2017	969065	462848	13300	2564	1056
2018	1065552	500484	10419	1992	812
2019	1135261	568282	11845	2034	829
2020	NA	NA	NA	NA	NA

No. of questions asked from different subjects in Prelims exam General Studies Paper-I (2011–2021)											
Subjects	2011	2012	2013	2014	2015	2016	2017	2018	2019	2020	2021
Ancient India & Culture	1	6	7	12	4	9	6	5	1	1	9
Medieval India and Culture	0	1	1	2	3	4	1	2	7	7	2
Modern India	9	12	11	11	11	12	13	14	7	9	10
Geography	19	16	20	18	17	7	8	8	10	5	13
Environment & Ecology	17	12	14	20	11	17	16	17	13	15	17
Indian Polity & Administration	10	15	17	12	10	5	22	10	14	11	20
Socio-economic Development	22	15	17	10	21	26	16	16	21	25	16
General Science	10	7	10	6	3	12	3	6	2	5	4
Science & Technology	6	6	3	8	10	17	3	8	4	4	7

No. of questions asked from different subjects in Mains Exam General Studies Paper-I to IV (2013–2021)									
Subjects	2013	2014	2015	2016	2017	2018	2019	2020	2021
Indian Heritage & Culture	4	4	2	2	1	2	2	5	4
Modern India & Indian National Movement	7	5	3	4	5	2	4	2	3
World History	4	2	2	1	1	0	1	0	0
India & World Geography	10	7	5	4	6	6	6	7	7
Indian Society & Social justice	12	8	17	12	9	9	8	11	11
Politics & Administration	10	7	9	10	9	9	10	11	9
International Relations	8	6	4	2	2	6	3	3	4
Socio-economic Development	16	14	9	8	14	11	13	8	9
Environment & Disaster Management	4	4	3	5	4	7	5	5	7
Science & Technology	6	3	5	6	4	4	4	3	2
International Security	66	5	5	3	5	3	4	4	4
Ethics, Aptitude & Integrity	8	8	8	8	8	6	6	6	6
Ethics, Aptitude & Integrity (Case Study)	6	6	6	6	6	12	12	12	12

Cut off Marks												
Category	**2018**			**2019**			**2020**			**2021**		
	Prelims	Mains	Final	Prelims	Mains	Final	Prelims	Mains	Final	Prelims	Mains	Final
General	98	774	982	98	752	961	92.51	736	944	87.54	745	953
OBC	96.6	732	938	95.34	718	925	89.12	698	907	84.85	707	910
EWS	-	-	-	90	696	909	77.55	687	894	80.14	713	916
SC	84	719	912	82	706	898	74.84	680	875	75.41	700	886
ST	83.34	719	912	77.34	699	893	68.71	682	876	70.71	700	883

❑

8

Interview Preparation

People who talk sweetly and only what is necessary are supreme.

—Acharya Chanakya

The civil service examination interview is the last frontier of a long and arduous process. The 275 marks which are allotted for the interview do not seem much when compared to the 1,750 marks allotted for the main examination; but the facts are completely different.

The Importance of the Interview

All the candidates who have been called for the interview are very close to reaching their goal (even if they do not attain top rank, they can be selected). In this stage, the marks allotted by the board are not only very important but also decide the final selection. Some candidates score more than 80–90 per cent marks in the interview while others may score only 30–40 per cent marks. Getting a high score in the interview enables you to attain a higher rank. The marks scored by you in this stage not only decide your selection or failure but also play an important role in getting your favoured or preferred appointment.

Do note that there is a difference of 300–350 marks amongst all the candidates who appear for the interview. This means that a fall of one point can drop your rank by 5–6 places. It is found that the difference in the marks of the top 100 candidates is quite substantial, whereas the difference is much less amongst the candidates in the middle and lower ranks. This means that in the interview the candidates must highlight their personality.

Every extra mark scored helps you to improve your rank. The interview gives you an opportunity to score those extra marks. But many candidates do not fully realise the importance of this stage and miss out on this golden opportunity, which can either reward or waste the hard work put in by you.

Normally, the interview is conducted in the month of March or April. In this stage, the candidates are judged through an interview by a board, consisting of five members. The UPSC constitutes six or seven such boards. Usually, a candidate is interviewed for half-an-hour.

Mock Interview

You can participate in mock interviews organised by coaching institutes, in case you feel relaxed. However, if you feel stressed facing a mock interview then do not participate in it at all.

The civil services interview is not an opportunity only to display a candidate's personality but also to improve and develop it to the level which is expected of a civil servant.

Personal Profile

Personal profile is an important step in the preparation for the civil services interview. It includes all the personal information which has been asked by the UPSC in the main examination application form. It includes details of your current job, your home state, your educational qualifications, your hobbies, your family background and your graduation subjects etc.

Personal profile is a document which lists your own achievements. It is, therefore, expected that you are fully aware of them. Mostly a board member starts the interview with a question from your personal profile, like asking your name or your educational qualifications. The idea is to make you feel relaxed. After this, questions to test your critical and analytical skills could be asked, like the challenges being faced by your home state or any issue related to your current job.

Why is the Interview Important?

In any competitive examination, the interview is very important as it tests the oral communication skills of the candidates. The persons conducting the interview are experienced, capable and specialists. Their function is to judge the candidates' ability for the distinguished career. They pay special attention to the following traits during the interview—candidate's personality, his interest towards the job, his sense of dedication and ability to understand the job requirements, test common knowledge and common sense, candidate's suitability and perception for the job. All the above qualities of the candidates are assessed and then marks are given. It is, therefore, necessary that one understands all the requirements clearly.

Personality

Personality has an extensive meaning. It must jointly combine the inner and overt qualities of a person, e.g., a person's looks and his stature, presentation, conversation style, response mannerism, knowledge of the subject and its expression, character, enthusiasm, willpower, courage and morality.

Some features like looks are god-gifted. But other qualities can be developed and improved by effort. Only an impressive personality can help you to succeed in the interview.

Interest and Dedication Towards Work

You must have a keen interest for the post for which you are aspiring. In the interview if it appears that you are not very keen for the job or you are there on account of some compulsion, then your success is doubtful.

Common Knowledge and Common Sense

Both are very helpful during the interview. There is difference in having common knowledge and being aware of the facts. Even if you are aware of the facts but are unable to use them at the opportune moment, then the knowledge you possess is useless. Having common knowledge enables you to answer appropriately on subjects which you have not learnt. It can be developed by knowledge. If you are instinctive, then you can create a favourable impression in the interview.

Ability According to the Post

Try to develop the qualities required for the post which you aspire. For example, an administrative post, technical post, legal post, financial controller, etc., all require specialisation and carry different responsibilities. Some of the required qualities may be common for all the posts but each of them also requires specialised skills, which you need to develop in advance.

Important Tips for the Interview

There are a few things which need to be taken care of during the course of the interview. Any slip up may lead to a negative impression.

- Do not enter the interview room without permission.
- While wishing the courtesy greetings, do not raise your hand.
- Take your seat only after you are asked to do so.
- Do say 'thank you' after you are asked to sit.
- Do not interfere in the interviewer's personal discussions, even if the matter concerns you.
- Do not place your personal belongings, e.g., briefcase, certificates, file, etc. on the interviewer's table.
- Do not enter or leave the room in a rush. It is a sign of nervousness. Enter and leave the room calmly.
- Do not speak unless questioned.
- In your replies, do not ridicule any person, organisation or political party.
- Do not express any doubt and uncertainty in front of the interviewers.
- In case you do not know the answer to any question, say so clearly. Do not try to guess, because they all know the right answer.
- Do not exaggerate about yourself.
- Do not argue unnecessarily.

- In case during the interview you cough or sneeze, use your handkerchief.
- Do not get into any religious controversy, say only what is humanitarian.
- In case you do not understand the question, then say 'pardon me please' and ask the question again. Do not try to answer without fully understanding the question.
- In the discussions, do use the salutations like 'Sir' or 'Mr.'
- During the discussion, do not express flattery.
- Remain polite and courteous and do not show arrogance or conceit.
- Do not appear to be discouraged or despondent during the interview.
- Remain calm and answer sensibly.

Some Facts

1. An unbelievable statement can cause lot of problems. So, think carefully before answering.
2. Whatever you say during discussion must be understood by the others clearly. Otherwise it will be meaningless.
3. Your statement must be based on your experience and belief. Only then will it reflect your self-confidence.
4. Writing is an art. To become proficient in it, practise writing using proper techniques.
5. Your written communication must have the determination of your thoughts, so prepare only after referring to the past record file.
6. Shakespeare had said—'Brevity is the soul of wisdom.' So, whatever you say or write, say it concisely. For it, your mind must be focused.
7. While writing your resume, take care of two things: (1) Include all the elements in the text, (2) Restrict the words to one-third.
8. In letter-writing, reconciliation is important. Its use depends on to whom you are writing.
9. In essay-writing, your fundamental ideas, imagination, knowledge on the subject and your ability to explain are assessed. So, be careful while selecting the subject.

10. In your speech, carry a sense of humour, but only if you have command over it.
11. While speaking, making use of the body language delivers twice as much impression on the audience. Therefore, it is a must to have the knowledge of the techniques as to when, where and which expression/ sign should be used.

Judge the Person in Front of You During the Interview

For your interview, the first step towards your success is your educational qualification. But apart from it, there are a few other things which can help you to succeed. One of them is 'pacing'. Try to act according to the mood of the interviewer. You will then be on the same frequency as the interviewer and chances of your success will improve. Normally, we like people who have a similar nature. This applies fully in case of one's career. A research conducted on this shows that during the interview the interviewers select such candidates whose nature is similar to their nature. The reason is that it becomes easy to work with them. Such people also adjust in a better manner. But it is difficult for the candidate to assess the interviewer's nature. However, experts provide a few tips. You can use them and overcome this difficulty.

The most important quality an interviewer desires is belief and trustworthiness. From your replies, it must seem that if any task is given to you, then you will fulfil it confidently and sincerely. That you are able, carry other people with you. In fact, without saying so, you should be able to convey the fact that you are like him (the interviewer); if you work with me, you will feel comfortable and you can fully trust me. As a matter of fact, this mantra will help you everywhere.

The simplest way to practise is that you also sit in the same manner as the interviewer, provided he is sitting formally. Also try to speak like him. The words and mannerisms should also be similar. Behaviourally, such an approach helps you a lot to create rapport with other people. You will also have to consider the frame of mind of the interviewer, because he expects that the person sitting in front of him is in the same mood. If it happens that the interviewer is in a serious mood, then you should not show enthusiasm or vice versa. Your enthusiasm or seriousness can complicate things. Just be mindful of the tenor of the discussion. Experts call it 'pacing' or maintain the pace of the person in front of you. In other words, it could be called feeling one's pulse.

One senior female officer Kavita says that if you are able to assess the mood of the interviewer, then you have won half the battle. Once you have convinced him that you fully understand what he is asking and you have the correct answer, then you can direct the interview in your desired direction. This is called establishing rapport with the interviewer, which may not be apparent, but it works like a dream.

Kavita says, "In case you wish to change someone's behaviour, then you must have the quality to change yourself as per the circumstances. Just ensure that the person realises that you understand him completely and then you can mould him as you wish."

Kavita narrates an incident—"Once a woman came to our office shouting violently. She was not prepared to listen to anyone. First I shouted back at her equally violently that what she was saying correct, and then I spoke to her about other things. Believe me, she calmed down in a short while. You can, thus, understand how effective pacing is and, in an interview, there is no question of raising your voice. All you have to do is to study the mood of the interviewer and reply politely. Using this technique, you can improve your normal life also. However, keep in mind that it is not easy to change yourself according to others. You need to exercise caution, do not go overboard in the process of aping."

Learn to Figure Out a Person

As we move out in the world to face the challenges armed with necessary energy and self-confidence, we meet people who may be structurally akin to us but have different nature and behaviour. It is said of successful people that they are able to figure out people who come in their contact. Are you also able to properly figure out people who come in contact with you?

A psychologist has said that no matter how much expertise we achieve, human nature will never cease to amaze us. But there is no need to be discouraged by this saying. This complex activity occurs very slowly and mostly depends on our own wisdom also. It is difficult to explain this vast subject in brief but a few tips can help us.

First, we must know about the nature of humans that he is a slave of the circumstances. Circumstances are mostly related to his needs. Any person, howsoever righteous and single-minded he might be, holds on to his principles only up to a certain limit. The number of people who stick to their principles is so limited that we can overlook them.

Some people are narrow-minded. It is not a shortcoming but a personal specialty. They never think positively. Mostly such people restrain themselves in a specified boundary and create difficulties, cause stress or strife for others and feel elated. It is easy to identify such people, but difficult to stay away from them because they leave no stone unturned to vitiate the atmosphere by their vile behaviour.

Some other people who come in our contact are adorable on account of their thinking and behaviour. They not only attain respect and success in the society but also inspire others to illuminate their lives. It is not difficult to identify them, but we need to change our thinking accordingly. Only then can we get close to them.

While some other people are even better. They even take up tasks in which they have no interest, not bothering about praise or criticism, with their full commitment. Such people are transparent and so is their working. The world is in great need of such people. People who change the course of history possess such nature.

In South Africa, a very successful billionaire in the business of gold and diamond was once asked by a person as to how he selected such confident, honest and skilled persons. His reply was, "That the type of business in which I am, this is a normal practice. To mine a few grams of gold, we have to dig tonnes of soil, yet the aim is to get gold and not soil. The same technique is used to select the people."

To be in the company of righteous people, to have people of good character at the workplace, it is not only a pleasure to see the devotion of dedicated people towards their objectives, but it is life's wealth. Like digging tonnes of soil is not the objective, only an activity; similarly, to avoid the company of people of loose character and thankless attitude should not be an objective but an activity. To get close to good people is difficult, not impossible, because their needs are similar. They also need good people. They are also removing their dust, as they also need to develop the good qualities. In this entire case, we must keep in mind one more fact: we should not depend on our experience but expand our horizon and gain from others' experiences also.

In the Interview Room

For civil services and different states PCS selection, there are three examinations – preliminary, main and interview. Amongst these, the interview is the last and most important examination, as the performance in it decides the final selection. Through the interview, the interview board assesses the candidate's complete personality. They want to ensure that the person, who is going to assume such vital responsibility, has a perfect personality, so that no complications arise in the future.

Make an honest assessment of your weaknesses before appearing for the interview and avoid nervousness, impatience, overeagerness and lying. Even though the interviewer's have your complete biodata, they ask questions from it, so prepare thoroughly all questions that could possibly be asked related to your biodata.

The questions on your subjects are already covered in the main examination. Questions on GS and GK are also asked. Answer them carefully.

After discussions with successful candidates, it has been found that the candidates are nervous when they appear before the interview board. Some of the candidates even start trembling. It portrays a weak personality. He says what he never intended to say and is unable to say what he intended to say. Many a candidates reply irrelevantly and only realise it after the board chairman asks him to leave or discusses the proceedings of the interview with his friends. So, avoid being nervous.

Impatience and overeagerness can result in wrong or incomplete answers and spoil the interview. Allow the interviewer to complete his question and answer only then and there. Not allowing the interviewer to complete his question is impoliteness. It is essential that you listen to the question carefully and answer it after due consideration.

Never try to lie during the interview. If you do not know the answer to any question, there is no point in lying or trying to bluff, as the interviewer is much more accomplished and knowledgeable than you. They will immediately guess your intention.

So it is best to apologise and clearly say that you do not know the answer. On several occasions, they answer it themselves, listen to it carefully and even if you have any doubts, do not raise them, because they are there not to teach you but to interview you.

After this is the time for question and answer. Normally, the questioning will start from your biodata. So, you must be prepared with the questions related to your biodata. For instance, if your birthday is on 2nd October, the question could be 'Why is this day famous in Indian history and what is its importance?' While you are answering this question, further related questions are framed by the interviewers to test the depth of your personality.

Similarly, if someone's birthplace is Rajgir in Nalanda district of Bihar, then the questioning can start from Nalanda and Rajgir; cover Nalanda University and even Jain/Budh religion.

Cover and prepare all such aspects in depth before the interview. Never give incorrect answers to these questions. If you do not know the answer say so clearly with due regret. Because if you give an incorrect answer, then you are likely to fall in the trap of related and subsequent questions, which will be framed by the highly intelligent persons sitting in front of you.

Some questions are asked from the candidate's optional subject, which deliver benefit to the common man's life. Since the depth of knowledge on the subject has already been tested in the main examination, such questions are rarely asked. But definitely there are questions on aspects of the subject which are socially and nationally important. So, prepare accordingly before the interview.

After this, there will be questions on GS and GK. Questions on the current events can be asked. How and/or did the events occur, what will be the implications of the events on the society and the nation and what are your reactions on them? Your ideas are judged from such questions. Such questions must be answered carefully and clearly to the satisfaction of the interviewers.

Towards the end of the interview, there definitely is a question relating to your post and the issues related to it. For instance the question can be 'Suppose that you are posted as an officer in a district and the district's Leader/Councilor/MLA/Minister approaches you with a problem, and for some reason misbehaves, abuses or even raises his hand on you, then what will you do in such a situation? Will you also react in a similar manner or settle it differently?' Such questions must be answered after due deliberation.

Alternatively, the question could be 'Suppose that you are the DM of a district and natural calamity like flood, earthquake, famine or dry spell occur, how will you deal with the crisis?' Such questions must be answered after due consideration and patiently. Through such questions, the interviewers test your endurance, presence of mind and ability to manage the crisis.

Remember that the object of the board is to test your ability and not to bother or disturb you. So answer the questions carefully and patiently.

If you keep in mind all the things discussed above, then you can face the interview easily and successfully. By observing all the above things, I was able to secure 225 marks out of 275 marks in the interview. It was the highest score for the Hindi medium for that year.

Sample Questions

Success in life is dependent quite a lot on our presentation capability. It is not necessary that you are a scholar of all the subjects, yet whatever knowledge you have of a subject, must be presented properly.

An ideal candidate is a salesman, who, during the interview presents his achievements in such a manner which impresses the interviewers.

It is not necessary the sample questions and answers given are comprehensive and most suitable. Candidates can prepare the questions and their answers best suited to them. The idea behind giving the sample questions and answers is to generally familiarise you with the techniques used during the interview.

We have presented the main questions and their correct answers from each field, which will enhance your knowledge and prove useful during the interview.

I am presenting below a mock interview, on the basis of which you can prepare for your interview. Some formalities which need to be observed when you enter the interview room are mentioned. These apply for all types of interviews.

Mock Interview

When a candidate's name is called, he opens the door slowly and asks for the permission to enter:

Sir/Madam, may I come in?

He enters the room on being granted the permission to enter. It is quite possible that there is a delay, but do not enter the room without getting the permission. In such a situation, he should keep waiting at the door. Sometimes, the interviewers deliberately delay granting the permission to assess him. In fact, they are testing the patience and civility of the candidate.

From the time you enter the room to the time you exit, you are being judged by the interviewers. So, think before you speak or act. After conclusion of the interview, while leaving the room, your behaviour must be civil and balanced. Your exit also counts. Just like, while entering, you need to take permission, say 'thank you' and rise gradually, lower your head a bit, restore the chair without making any sound and leave. Also make sure that while opening or closing the door, there is no noise. After leaving the room, if you have to speak to anyone, make sure that you are sufficiently distant and your voice will not be heard by the interviewers.

Sample Interview – One

Candidate Sandeep Rai has been called for the interview. He is sitting outside the room with other candidates. On being called by the peon, he proceeds to the interview room. At the door, he halts and seeks permission to enter and, on being granted permission, he enters the room.

Sandeep bows and wishes all the interviewers and stands in front of the table.

Interviewer: Please sit.

Sandeep: 'Thank you Sir!' and sits down on the chair. The interview carries on for quite some time. After that—

Interviewer: Thank you Mr. Rai, you may leave now.

Sandeep: Thank you Sir!

Sandeep gets up from the chair, wishes all the members and leaves the room.

Sample Interview – Two

Question: Please tell us about yourself.

Answer: Sir, my name is Rajesh. My father Shri Suresh Kumar Verma works in the Electricity department. I have secured B.Sc. degree from Delhi University. I not only hope but am sure that I, with my devotion for my duty, will prove to be a deserving candidate.

Question: What is your life's aim?

Answer: Sir, every person desires to occupy a senior post. He desires for all the worldly happiness and comforts. I am not different from those persons. But I wish to attain the post with my devotion to duty, honesty and hard work.

Question: What is the meaning of success in your life?

Answer: Any person's success depends on his hard work, devotion and effort. I believe that you succeed in life only when you achieve your aim. Everyone has different aims. So the meaning of success is also different for different persons.

Question: Which type of people do you dislike?

Answer: Sir, I prefer to stay away from the company of people who do not stick to their words. I have met such people and am able to identify them easily.

Question: English is very popular now; our youth are adopting the English language and culture. What is your opinion?

Answer: In our country, English is being blindly adopted. We are moving away from our language and culture. Our youth considers foreign languages and literature superior. Their life-style and life's philosophy is influencing us beyond our country's needs. This is distancing us from our culture. We have started considering it as an honour, which, I think, is wrong.

Question: Is it wrong to learn other's language and culture?

Answer: No Sir, it is perhaps not wrong to learn from others. We must definitely learn from others, but we must always keep in mind that our background does not change on account of the knowledge. Our culture is deep-rooted and has a lot of specialities. It is great; it is much more ancient and proven than any other culture. Other civilisations and cultures have disappeared but our civilisation and culture still exist. We must adopt the superior elements from it and make them the basis of our life.

Question: Our country has been guided by Saints-Mahatmas and Rishis-Munis. Is it possible to achieve the welfare of the society by following the path of worship. What do you think?

Answer: Our country's Saints-Mahatmas have given guidance to the world, but it is also a fact that worship cannot solve the problems of the materialistic world, but it does show the way to solve the problems. Saints like Tulsidas,

Kabirdas, Kalidas, Surdas, etc., through the path of worship, have illuminated our lives with knowledge, Karma (work) and Adhyatma (knowledge relating to God and soul), that light is still illuminating our lives. They have stressed on the coordination of all these things which play an important role in character building. Any person with a good character can meet any challenge with ease and contribute in the welfare of the society and country.

Question: What is your opinion on 'Reservation'?

Answer: It is a difficult issue. It seems necessary as some sections of our society are backward. They might have talent but have not got adequate opportunities to develop. Their state can improve through reservation, the extent of which has been specified in the constitution. It should be implemented as specified in the constitution and not according to the demands of national leaders for their vested interests or their vote bank politics.

Question: Do you agree that for the same work women be paid less than men?

Answer: Sir, I do not agree that women be paid less than men for the same work. Our constitution specifies that everyone must be paid the same wages for the same work. Unfortunately, the private companies are not following this regulation, but it has been implemented by the public sector undertakings and in government jobs, the results of which are evident to us.

Question: What is the meaning of 'Recession' and how does it impact the economy?

Answer: Recession means slowing down of the economy; it occurs when the demand is less than the production. In such a state, the shortage of money reduces the purchasing capacity of the people and the goods produced remain unsold. It leads to closure of industry and unemployment. In the decade of 1930, there was worldwide recession and all the countries were affected.

Question: What is the meaning of deficit financing?

Answer: When the government's budget shows a loss, that is when its income is less than the expenditure, then the government borrows from the central bank or prints more currency note to cover the deficit, this arrangement is called deficit financing. It is considered right only if it is controlled or limited. The consequences are not good for any country if it becomes a regular practice.

Question: What is bridge loan?

Answer: To raise capital for the business, companies usually issue fresh shares or debentures. This process normally takes about three months. To meet the financial requirements of the business for the intervening period, the companies raise loans from the banks. This type of loan is called 'bridge loan'.

Question: What is the meaning of poverty?

Answer: Poverty is defined as the state which is below the average minimum social existence level. According to the task-force set up by the planning commission to study the minimum needs and effective consumption—when the consumption is less than 2,400 calories in the rural areas and less than 2,100 calories in the urban areas per person, the specified yardstick, that state is defined as poverty.

Question: What are the meanings of gross domestic product and gross national product?

Answer: Gross domestic product is the total market or monetary value of all the final goods or services produced in a country over a specified period, usually a year. Gross national product is the total value of all final goods and services produced within a nation in a particular year, plus income earned by its citizens (including income of those located abroad), minus income of non-residents located in that country.

Question: What is your understanding of national income?

Answer: It is the monetary value of all the goods and services produced in the country, without duplicating, during a particular period. At current value it is called net national income. It can be represented by the following formulas:

- National income minus net national product (at cost price)
- Net national product at market prices minus indirect tax subsidy

- Gross domestic product at market prices net of foreign income minus depreciation minus indirect tax subsidy.

Question: Explain the meaning of currency inflation?

Answer: Currency inflation is a state where restricting or controlling the currency supply is beneficial for an underdeveloped economy. Though it encourages production increase, but currency inflation beyond a certain limit is damaging. To control the currency inflation temporarily, the currency supply can be restricted.

Question: What is the implication of depreciation in the economy?

Answer: If the exchange rate of a currency is intentionally depreciated as compared to other currencies, then it is called currency depreciation. The depreciation is done by the government considering the circumstances.

Question: What is the effect of demonetisation on the economy? Does it harm the country?

Answer: When black money grows, it becomes a threat to the economy. To overcome this threat, demonetisation of the currency is resorted to. Under this, some old currency denomination notes are extinguished and new currency notes are introduced. People who have black money do not dare to exchange the currency and it becomes useless. It does not harm the economy; on the contrary, it benefits the economy by controlling inflation.

Question: What are the merits of the Indian Constitution?

Answer: The Indian constitution is the abstract of all constitutions of the world:

- The merger of the princely provinces.
- Belief in the powers of the people.
- Democratic form of government.
- Focus on unity and integration of the country.
- Equality and justice for all the citizens.
- Provisions for the backward classes.
- Respect for all religions.

Question: What are fundamental rights of the citizens?

Answer: Our main fundamental rights are:

- Right to equality.
- Right against suppression.
- Right to independence.
- Right to education and culture.
- Right to religious freedom.
- Right to seek constitutional remedy.
- Right to freedom of speech.

Question: What is the meaning of policy directive principles?

Answer: They are guidelines to the central and state governments of India to be kept in mind while framing laws and policies. These principles are not enforceable by any court, but are considered fundamental in the governance of the country, making it the duty of the State to apply these principles in making laws to establish a just society in the country. Some of these are:

- State will strive to promote the welfare of the people.
- Provide adequate means of livelihood for all citizens; men and women will be paid same wages for same work.
- State shall work towards reducing economic inequality.
- State shall work to prevent concentration of wealth in a few hands.
- Promotion of cottage industries.
- Prohibit intoxicating drinks and drugs that are injurious to health.
- Child abuse and exploitation of workers will be prevented.
- Secure a uniform civil code for all citizens.
- Organise village panchayats.
- Prohibit slaughter of cows, calves, and milch and draught cattle.
- Strive for promotion and maintenance of international peace and security.

Question: What do general elections mean? When are they held?

Answer: General elections are held every five years to elect members of the parliament. Any citizen of India who is 18 years old or more has the right to vote, irrespective of religion, caste, lineage etc.

Question: What is Indian Election Commission?

Answer: It is responsible for conducting all the elections in the country for the parliament, state legislatures, the President and other elections as specified in the constitution. Preparing the voters list, notifying, supervising, directing and controlling the elections also come under its purview.

Question: What do Rajya Sabha and Lok Sabha mean?

Answer: They are the two houses of Parliament. Rajya Sabha has 250 members. They are representatives from the states and the union territories. Two representatives are nominated by the President, from those who have made a mark from the fields of arts, literature, culture, science or social service. Two-thirds of its members retire every two years. It is the upper house of the parliament. Lok Sabha is the lower house of the parliament in which the representatives are elected by the people. It has a maximum of 545 members, 525 from the states and 20 from the union territories (UT). It has a tenure of 5 years.

Question: What is the authority of the President?

Answer: President is the head of the state and has many different types of powers. The President of India has extensive powers to handle crisis and emergency situations. Some of them are:

Executive powers.

Constitutional powers.

Financial powers.

Legal powers.

Political powers.

Emergency powers.

Question: What do you know about the Supreme Court?

Answer: The judges of the Supreme Court are appointed by the President in consultation with the Chief Justice of the Supreme Court and the Governor. Their term is up to the age of 62.

Question: Is the Indian economy a rural and agriculture-based economy?

Answer: The Indian economy is a rudimentary and developing economy. Even 60 years after independence, nearly 58 per cent of the work force is engaged in agriculture. So, it can be concluded that the Indian economy is primarily agriculture-based. Though its contribution to the gross domestic product is only 22 per cent.

Question: It is said that the Indian economy is a mixed economy. What is your opinion?

Answer: Mixed economy means the co-existence of private sector and public sector undertakings. India has adopted this economy in the post-independence era, so that its socialistic objectives can be fulfilled. The government has invested nearly 45 per cent capital in the public sector over all the plan periods, but even today the private sector holds nearly 80 per cent in the production sources and resources. In spite of all the liberalisation, the Indian economy is headed towards capitalistic economy.

Question: Please tell in brief the meaning of 'renaissance.'

Answer: It refers to 'reawakening or reawareness.' It is the resurgence of ideas and culture of earlier periods. In Europe people became interested in ideas and culture of ancient Greece and Rome from the 15th century to 17th century. It is considered as the golden era of literature, art and painting, etc.

Expectations from the Candidates

We have earlier discussed the points which a candidate must take care of during the interview. We now discuss this from the perspective of the interviewer, that is, what points he looks for in the candidate.

The candidate's selection depends on what the interviewer is looking for in the candidate. The interviewer's sights remain focused on the candidate from the time he enters the interview room to the time he departs. The interviewer studies in depth the candidate's character, intelligence, ingenuity, nature, alertness, common sense, tolerance, patience, amiability, thinking ability and his/her family's condition.

They also test his eagerness to learn about new things. Normally, the interviewer pays special attention to the possibility of the candidate building his career in the field in which he is proficient.

During the discussion, the interviewers also try to determine if the candidate is trying to hide something. They prefer honest and truthful candidates. They also consider the candidate's expression capability and his behaviour.

Interviewers prefer candidates who are obedient, who understand their responsibilities, are dedicated and talk sweetly. Apart from all these considerations the candidate must also be healthy.

The interviewers give preference to candidates who are ambitious to attain senior position through dedicated work. They dislike oversmart candidates.

They test the dynamism and vision of the candidates. They keep a close watch on questions which unnerve him and on questions on which he maintains his mental balance.

The interviewers do not like the candidates who are uncertain in his approach and closely observe how he handles himself in different situations. They note the candidate's earnestness and dedication towards his work. They prefer candidates who have good habits and are well groomed. They dislike candidates who are blunt and talk excessively.

The interviewers observe the candidate's vocabulary understanding ability. They also judge if the candidate is quick-witted and whether he is able to answer quickly. On their part, they make sure that the candidate feels relaxed.

They study whether the candidate is suitable and has the capability. They expect that the candidate has good command over the languages he/she knows.

Before selecting the candidate, the interviewers consider the following points:

1. Intelligence
2. Understanding
3. Self-confidence
4. Expressibility of ideas
5. Character
6. Capability to explain
7. Academic record
8. Grooming
9. Health

Success Tips for the Interview

Hard work is the key to success. When you dedicate yourself in any task, the results are bound to be positive. Everyone wants to be employed after completing studies, but only some are selected. If we follow certain things, then we can succeed in every field. If you wish to succeed in the interview, then follow the following simple points:

Keep track of time

It is very important to keep track of time. Try to reach everywhere a little bit earlier. This habit will help you to succeed. It is important that you reach for the interview ahead of time. If you reach earlier, then you can talk to the other candidates and find out about the interview panel and the probable questions and adjust yourself mentally.

Pay attention to your attire

Pay special attention to your attire for the interview. Wear neat, clean and well-ironed formal clothes. Your hair should be well groomed. Female candidates should duly tie their hair so that there is no need to settle them repeatedly.

Go well prepared

Before you go for the interview, find out all you can about the job. Keep all your documents properly organised in a folder.

During the interview, present the documents asked for; do not panic and give some other document by mistake. Before the interview do not think about extraneous things. Only think about the probable questions, so that, when asked, you can answer them confidently.

Listen to the interviewer with full attention

Be focused during the interview. Listen to every question carefully, so that there is no need for the question to be repeated. Doing so will affect your impression. In many instances, the candidate, in his enthusiasm, starts answering it even before the question is completed. This leaves a bad impression. Do not feel nervous. If you have prepared properly, you will definitely succeed.

Do not lie

If you do not know the answer to any question, avoid answering it and say so, instead of trying to show as if you know the answer. Otherwise, your chances of selection will become very slim.

Maintain a positive attitude

Do not criticise anyone under any circumstance. Also do not brag about yourself, let the interviewer decide.

Your posture

Maintain a relaxed posture. Do not fidget or repeatedly wipe your sweat. Maintaining a mild smile is very effective.

Do not raise your voice

Do not reply in a loud voice or murmur so that the interviewer is unable to hear you. Answer normally in a sweet tone. As far as possible, use your words carefully. Do not keep on speaking incessantly. Allow the interviewer also to speak.

Address the board

If there are two or more than two members in the board, several types of questions will be asked. It is best if you address everyone while answering, answer politely and involve everyone.

Do not argue

During the interview, do not argue, as it does not establish either your self-confidence or your knowledge. You can convince the interviewer about your talent by self-confidence and politeness and not by arguing. So, avoid controversy and argument.

Some Considerations

There are three examinations for the civil services and state PCS—preliminary, main and interview. Of these, interview is the last one and is perhaps the most important one. So, it carries a lot of weight in the final selection. In fact, the board assesses the complete personality of the candidate through the interview. They want to ensure that the person, who is going to shoulder such an important responsibility, has a perfect personality and no problems arise in the future.

Before appearing for the interview, you need to do an honest assessment of your weaknesses like nervousness, impatience, overenthusiasm, lying, etc. and overcome them. Even though the interview board has your complete biodata, yet they ask you questions related to it. So, you must prepare answers to all the possible questions related to it.

If you take care of all the above points, then you can face the interview board within a relaxed frame of mind and perform well.

An Interview Exercise

Ruchika: May I come in Sir?

Reply: Please come in, sit.

Ruchika: Thank you Sir, Good morning Sir.

Question: Ruchika, you completed your school and college education from Delhi. You were born and brought up here. So, you can be called a Delhiite. Please tell us what you think about this city? What do you like and dislike about this city?

Ruchika: Sir, Delhi is the capital city of India. It has its own rich history, social impact and a growing economy. Apart from this, it has many reputed academic institutions, ultra modern metro transportation and historic monuments, which make it a world-class city. Asian Games have been held here twice. In spite of all these good points, uncontrolled pollution, chaotic traffic, worst law and order situation, and administration bother me a lot.

Question: Who all are responsible for Delhi's pollution? How can this pollution be controlled?

Ruchika: Delhi's pollution has reached to an alarming level, for which the vehicles, industry and homes are responsible. The main pollutants are the vehicles. Delhi has lakhs of private and public vehicles. It has more vehicles than all the vehicles in the three metros (Chennai, Mumbai and Kolkata) put together. To control the pollution, we need to introduce ecologically friendly modern transportation. The metro is the right step in this direction. There is also the need to improve the functioning of the public transportation system, so that more people can use it conveniently instead of their private vehicles. Introduction of Mono Rail, electrically operated buses, car pools etc. must be given priority.

Question: Ruchika, what is G-77? What is its stance on climate change and global warming? What is India's stance?

Ruchika: G-77 is a group of world's developing nations. Even though this group is not as powerful as the other groups of the United Nations, yet it is the largest group in United Nations to promote the interests of the developing nations. It has offices in various cities of the world, of which the ones in Geneva, Nairobi, Rome, Vienna and Washington DC are main. This group was formed by 77 nations in 1964. Over time, more nations have joined as members. Currently, its strength is 130, but, considering its historic relevance, it continues to be called G-77. India is also its member. On the issue of climate change and global warming, its stance is that the developed nations are largely responsible for it and should bear the responsibility of introducing the emission norms and implementing them. The developing nations should not be burdened with it.

Question: You have been playing hockey. Please tell when was the last time India's women's hockey team won a major tournament.

Ruchika: Sir, I do not know.

Question: What do you know about the 'sub-prime crisis?'

Ruchika: Sir, in America, sub-prime is a category of loan. In America, the loans are categorised based on the risk profile. The loan with the least risk is called prime loan. It has the least possibility of default. The next category with higher risk is called Alt-A loan. The loan with the highest risk is called sub-prime loan and carries the highest interest rate. The financers do not bother much about the borrower's record. It is given against collateral mortgage. The American financial institutions advanced huge amount of loans under this category. It started with the American housing market boom. The prices of real estate were skyrocketing. The Americans could raise loan by mortgaging their own homes to finance construction of new homes and earn a decent profit by selling it. The financial institutions were also making handsome profits. Even if the borrowers were unable to repay the loan, the institutions would sell the mortgaged property and realise their loan. This led to the tremendous increase in the number of borrowers. By 2005, they had advanced 635 billion dollars as loans. By 2007, this figure reached 10 trillion dollars. Since the rate of interest was demand-dependent, as the number of borrowers increased, the rates of interest also rose. However, the construction of new homes on this unprecedented scale dipped the property prices. The demand slipped. It became difficult to sell the property and the owners were forced to sell them at much lower prices. Under these circumstances, the borrowers were unable to repay the loan. Since the loans had been raised by mortgaging their old homes, they could not sell them also. This resulted in the rise in the number of defaulters. Eventually, the financial institutions were the losers. Due to the significant fall in the property prices, the institutions could not fully recover the loan amount. The housing industry crisis remained a major issue of the American economy for the next 4–5 years; the sub-prime crisis started in

2006. More than 100 financial institutions declared bankruptcy. A section of the American intellectuals and media raised this issue repeatedly, but the government did not take it seriously. On 15th August, 2007, sub-prime loans collapsed.

With this reply, Ruchika's interview concluded. Her interview went very well. She answered almost all the questions raised by the board with full confidence, particularly those questions which sought her ideas and opinions. She gave logical answers and fully satisfied the board.

Summary

It is usually seen that even experienced persons become nervous at the very thought of facing an interview. It is, therefore, natural for a first-timer to be nervous at the thought of facing an interview. But if we prepare in advance, then we can face the interview successfully. Develop your self-confidence. Reply to the questions without undue haste. Answer succinctly in brief. Avoid unnecessarily prolonging your answers. Try to bring out your ability and intelligence in the answers.

Several candidates become nervous due to the lack of self-confidence and lose the opportunity to succeed. The most important consideration to succeed in the interview is your self-confidence. Due to the lack of self-confidence, even talented candidates are unable to properly bring out their ability, knowledge and learning in front of the interview board.

The fear of failing or lack of confidence is usually more pronounced in candidates who have been unsuccessful previously. But they should bear in mind the fact that in this world, there is not a single person who has never faced failure, even though he might have become extremely successful in the future. So, every candidate must maintain his morale and face the interview with full confidence. It is certain that you shall be successful. Any mental block will prevent you from achieving your goal.

The preparation for the interview cannot be done in a day, a night or even in a week, as is done by many present-day candidates. It is required that you prepare replies to all questions which are likely to be asked and memorise them. Read all the competition magazines in Hindi and English, which cover all the latest events regularly. Also go through the social and political newspapers and magazines. Apart from this, familiarise yourself with the latest national, international social, political, scientific and economic events.

Attend the interview with the positive feeling that the time has come to present and prove the hard work and preparation put in over a long period of time.

Frequently Asked Questions

The following questions are frequently asked during the interview:

- In spite of your technical background, why do you want to join the civil services?
- What are your hobbies?
- What will you do if you are not selected?
- Please discuss any weakness which you have.
- What is your father's profession?
- What do your brothers and sisters do?
- How do you spend your free time?
- What is your future planning?

Also remember some more points. In the application form, the candidate is required to furnish details about his interest and participation in sports. Do not give the name of a sport which you have never played or mention a hobby of which you have no idea, just to impress the interviewers. Otherwise, you will be exposed after a few questions and thus create a negative impression. Not having a special hobby is not a disqualification. If you have listed a sport in your biodata, then learn about the various forms of the game, the names of the well-known players of the game (male as well as female), India's achievements in the game and suggestions for improving the game, etc. You can be questioned on all these aspects and more. If you have named a special interest, then you can be asked to name the books which you have read? Who are your favourite authors? Changes which have taken place in the writings over time.

Be punctual. Do not keep preparing and sleep late on the eve of the interview. Sleep on time so that you wake up fresh in the morning.

Sometimes, the interviewers may behave strangely. Do not be disturbed by it. For instance, many times, it happens that even if you have answered a question correctly, the question is asked again. In such a situation, remain firm on your reply.

In the interview room, smoking, eating *pan masala* (betel mixture), scratching your head, flexing your fingers, yawning, rolling your *mustaches*, poking your nose and biting your nails, etc. leave a bad impression on the interviewers.

As far as possible, brush up your general knowledge. Thereafter, take care of the following points:

- Go through two newspapers every day.
- Have group discussion with friends on different topics and current affairs, in detail, on all the aspects and issues. Correct the pronunciation deficiencies during the discussion.
- Give satisfactory answers to questions of your special interest.
- Get detailed knowledge on the questions related to your life circle and practise the answers.
- Prepare answers to the likely questions that may be asked related to your background.
- Seek detailed knowledge of the effects of national, international, trade and financial events on the Indian economy.

Some Important Tips for the Interview Day

- Candidates must remain physically and mentally relaxed; adopt a positive and cheerful outlook.
- Must maintain proper and disciplined behaviour at the interview site.
- Must read that day's newspaper.
- Drink some water before entering the interview room.
- While entering the interview room, smile and wish all the board members.

- Sit comfortably, looking alert. Smile and look at all the board members, then rest your sights on the board chairman expectantly.

Sometimes they may ask you a hypothetical question like—if your senior officer turns out to be short-tempered and impatient, would you like to work under him?

Actually, it is a tricky question. It is obvious that no one would like to work under a short-tempered and impatient officer, but if your answer is 'no', then you would be considered unfit. If your answer is 'yes', then you could be considered over-confident.

It is very difficult to guess what the interviewer's next question could be. Several times they may generate a peculiar question from your reply. For instance, if your name is Gopal Krishan Avdhiya, he may ask you 'Gopal also means Krishan and Krishan is any way Krishan, so how come you are Krishan twice?'

Your answer could be, Sir, in my name 'Krishan' is a noun, whereas Gopal is an adjective. It describes the noun. 'Gopal Krishan' means 'the caretaker of cows'. So, I am not Krishan twice but only once.

If you are asked 'What would you like to be—a neckless giraffe or a trunkless elephant?' Or 'How much time would be required to move an average-sized mountain by one kilometre?' Then what can you answer?

It is true that during the interview such irrelevant questions are asked which have no bearing on the service. Howsoever peculiar the questions might be, the interviewers are not fools. They do have a purpose behind such questions. By asking such peculiar questions, they might be testing your mentality or seeking any latent talent in you. It is important for the interviewer to find out how you answer such questions, the answer is not important. He also is aware that such questions have no meaningful answers. The interviewer tries to assess your personality based on how you react to such questions. It is also a fact that such questions are asked to filter the number of candidates. So, it is important for you to answer the question after due consideration, maintaining your restraint.

Principle Mantra (Advice)

The first five minutes of the interview are most important. In most cases, your marks are decided during this period. So, remain completely relaxed and answer with your natural smile. You can get good marks by maintaining a polite stance and patiently answering to the point.

❑

9

Some Success Stories

Focussing on your aim leads to success.

—Swami Vivekananda

Success stories often inspire us. In this chapter, the experiences of some successful civil service candidates have been narrated. They provide excellent guidance to the candidates preparing for the civil service examination.

Your Struggle Itself is Success

The story of Navin Kumar Jha who was selected for Civil Services, is a story of struggle and success. Navin, who was selected in the third attempt, believes that if you belong to an ordinary family, have an ordinary background, do not have sufficient resources and do not get through in the first attempt, do not be disheartened. UPSC provides you sufficient opportunities to succeed. All you need is patience and hard work.

Navin, who was selected as an officer of the Railways, comes from a middle-class family and accepted all the challenges to succeed. To make up for the lack of resources, he gave tuitions to children. According to him, "My family has contributed a lot to my success, particularly my elder brother who is an export manager in a private company. My financial condition was not too good. I hail from a rural background. However, the members of my family supported me throughout my journey."

In the first attempt, Navin cleared the Preliminary examination, in the second attempt he went up to the stage of Interview and, in the third attempt, his persistence paid and he was selected. However, his rank was not good enough to secure him an IAS officer's post. Navin is engaged in further preparations even after being selected. He believes that poverty and lack of resources do not necessarily hinder a person's progress; they can actually be a source of inspiration. If you have the required determination to make it in the Civil Services Examination, no challenge or difficulty can stop you and you are bound to succeed.

Nurse Becomes an IAS Officer

A farmer in Kerala aspired that his daughter should become an IAS officer. To fulfil it, he gave the best of education to his daughters and one of them fulfilled his dream.

The girl who achieved the feat is Anniez Kanmani Joy, who succeeded in clearing the 2012 Civil Services Examination. Joy not only cleared the examinations, but also secured 65th rank. This was actually Joy's second success. She had passed the examination in 2011 also, but her rank was 580. On the basis of this she was selected for the Indian Accounts Service and was undergoing Officer's training

What inspired her to become an IAS Officer? In reply to this question, Anniez says, "From childhood itself my father had inspired me but I never prepared for it. I prepared for it only after completing my nursing internship."

Anniez is the first nurse to succeed in the Civil Services Examination. She never knew that she would be the first nurse to do so. She says, "While preparing for the examination, I thought of seeking help from a nurse who had become an IAS Officer, but I couldn't find anyone. It was only after I passed the examinations that I came to know that before me no nurse had become an IAS Officer."

"A rural background does not have much bearing. What matters is how strong you are. In any case, I come from Kerala, where education is considered very important. That a village girl achieved so much may seem a big thing for you but to me it all feels like a normal thing."

What did her father say on hearing the news? Anniez replied, "When I informed him over phone, he was speechless. But I could feel his immense happiness."

Anniez told another important thing, "My father believed that education is the real wealth that a father can give to his daughter. Even though we are farmers, he made sure that I got the best education." It is common practice in Kerala that the parents compulsorily send their children to school.

Anniez says that in the last two years, she studied for 9 hours every day. When she was asked whether she missed anything in the last two years, she said, "Maybe I did miss a few festivals and occasions to meet my relatives and friends, but I don't think I missed much."

From a Labourer to an IAS Officer

One day a kid was working at a place where famine relief work was being carried out. Some officials came by to inspect the work. The kid learned that the report would be submitted to the Collector, the highest official. The kid made up his mind, there and then, to become a Collector.

Even though it is a very brief but a very inspiring struggle story of 30-year-old Hukmaram Choudhury, who secured 110th rank in the UPSC examination. He was the first IAS officer of his village.

Hailing from a very small village Bherunda in Nagaur, Hukmaram says that since his father was an asthma patient, he had to shoulder the responsibility of looking after the family from an early age.

Hukmaram used to attend school as well as look after the fields and work as a labourer during the summer vacations. He did not accept defeat even while facing adverse circumstances. After passing his 12th class and completing college, he gave tuitions to the children of his village. He also completed his M.Sc.

By the time he completed his graduation, Hukmaram was selected as a teacher, but his aim was to become an IAS officer. He stayed in Delhi for a year and prepared for the examination and his efforts bore fruits. When the villagers came to know that he had become an IAS officer, they took out a procession in the village in his honour.

Hukmaram says, "To achieve one's aim, one must work hard honestly." Hukmaram has set an example for the youth. Howsoever tough the journey to your objective might be, to reach there, a lot of hard work has to be put in.

If You are Determined

At the tender age of 18, in spite of the fact that his father, who was a school teacher, was killed by terrorists, Shah Faizal did not lose heart. Out of 4 lakh and 93 thousand candidates, who had applied for the Preliminary examinations, he topped the list of 875 candidates, who were finally selected for the Civil Services. He not only paid a fitting tribute to his father, but to also his mother who was also a school teacher and fulfilled her dreams.

Explaining the secret of his topping the merit list, he said "I wanted to end the long standing myth that Kashmiris could not qualify this examination. By qualifying in the first attempt, I have shattered this myth."

Speaking on the mantra for success, Faizal says, "Concentration and dedication have been my main mantra. I would like to give five tips to the aspirants, namely command over language, maintain a balanced expression, develop creativity, expand your knowledge and hold unbiased view on issues."

There is maximum infiltration of terrorists from the Kupwara district in Jammu and Kashmir. Faizal was born on May 17, 1983 in Shogam-Lolab village of this district. From the beginning, Faizal was a meritorious student and completed his 10th standard with distinction from Government High School in Shogam. Then he passed his 12th standard from Tidal Bisco School, where he secured 485 marks out of 500. His father Gulam Rasool was a teacher in government school and was living a contented life with his wife, two sons and a daughter.

Suddenly, one day, it seemed as if someone had cast an evil spell on their happiness. Their happiness was converted into gloom on the night of July 3, 2002, when terrorists knocked on their door and demanded food and shelter. Gulam Rasool kept pleading with the terrorists to excuse him, as his son was preparing for the medical entrance examination, but they did not pay heed to his pleas. Rasool was shot dead in front of his family. The members of the family were so shaken by the incident that they left Shogam and shifted to Srinagar.

Faizal was scheduled to take the medical entrance examination a day after his father's murder. He took the examination and surprised everyone by clearing it. After completing his MBBS from Srinagar's Sher-e-Kashmir Institute of Medical Science College, Faizal decided against doing a house job. During this time, he was also actively involved in the Right to Information (RTI) campaign.

Faizal believed that if you want to bring about changes in the system, you must join the Civil Services. His mother, who was a school teacher in a government school, says, "My son had an amazing determination to become an IAS officer. He used to ask me why I was admitted to a medical college? I used to reply that I wanted to ensure a secure future for him. But I am happy that he has fulfilled his dream."

Faizal also topped the Civil Services Examination coaching conducted by Kashmir University. After passing the preliminary examination in 2009, Faizal moved to Delhi to prepare for the main examination.

On being asked as to what special strategy he followed to top the IAS merit list, in reply, Faizal said, "I always believed there was no short cut to success. You must know your objective and work hard honestly to achieve it. I did not study for long hours, but whatever I studied, I did with full concentration. I never studied for long periods at a stretch. I believed that I needed some entertainment also. So, I listened to Kashmiri music and Nusrat Fateh Ali Khan."

When Faizal, who has done his MBBS from Srinagar's Sher-e-Kashmir Institute of Medical Science College, was asked why he decided to leave the medical profession and join the Civil Services, he says, "I wanted to serve the people. Of course, you can do that in the medical profession as well, but the scope is limited. Moreover, after you join the civil services, you can frame policies by keeping the welfare of the people in mind and the scope to work for the people is unlimited."

He further adds, "My subject in the Preliminary examinations was Public Administration, while in the Main examination, I opted for Public Administration and Urdu Literature. During the preparation, I concentrated on comprehensive studies and also focused on language, pronunciation and communication skills. Apart from this, whatever I studied, I kept in mind the correlation in all the subjects." As to why he opted for a fresh subject instead of MBBS subject, he says, "Since my aim was IAS, so I thought public administration would be more appropriate. Since I had to work with and among people, this subject was relevant in all respects. Moreover, I have an emotional connect with Urdu Literature. Faiz Ahmad Faiz and Iqbal are my favourite *shayars* (Urdu poets)."

Derived Inspiration from Suffering

Even if you are living amid poverty in thatched huts, in the first attempt itself, you can secure a good rank in the civil services examination. The person, who is a vivid example of this, is 21 years old Harish Chandra from Delhi , who prepared for the examination in the college library, park and lawn and secured 309th rank.

He says, "I grew up amid poverty. I was brought up by my mother who was a housemaid and my father who was a daily-wage labourer. Ever since I came of age, I was extremely pained to see the wretched condition of my parents and house. Even though I did dream of a miracle happening, after passing my 12th standard examination, when I joined Hindu College, it seemed as if my life had changed dramatically. In a manner, this was the turning point in my life. In fact, from the very beginning, I found the atmosphere of Hindu College very conducive for studies. It boosted up my self-confidence immensely and I started thinking about becoming an IAS Officer."

Harish continues, "Until class X, in addition to studying, I used to work in a store. So, I could not study properly and got poor marks. After my admission in 12th class, I gave up the stores job and started giving tuitions. This helped me and I secured 80% marks in the class XII examination.

My class fellow in college Ashu Mishra, who was blind but determined, opened my eyes. He had a positive approach and was able to move ahead. Before I met him, I had an inferiority complex. I was inspired by him and decided to develop myself. I was also impressed by the success of a rickshaw-puller's son, Govind Jaiswal and realised that even an ordinary person by his efforts can become an IAS Officer. In addition, I got full support from my parents and teachers."

"Due to poor financial condition, I earmarked my goals in parts and set about to achieve them. First, I consolidated my position in my subjects. This gave me confidence. I was getting scholarship from the university. So I was able to continue my studies without much difficulty. My parent's support encouraged me to be different. I completed my BA with full devotion and secured 64% marks. My subjects were political science and philosophy. I decided to opt for these two subjects to become an IAS Officer. Since I was underage to appear for the IAS examination, I completed my MA and cleared the JRF examination in the first attempt."

"I used to study for 8–10 hours every day for the IAS examination. I had started studying seriously one year before the examination. I first studied the question papers of the past years properly and started preparing accordingly. I then divided my time for studying the subjects. I went through the newspapers daily which helped me improve my current affairs' knowledge. I believed that coaching was not essential to succeed in the civil services examination. Coaching could only provide a direction. Success could only be achieved by one's own efforts. I got directions from Patanjali IAS Coaching for preparing philosophy and could score good marks."

Success in First Attempt

Harish says, "This was my first attempt. After the preliminary examination, I started preparing for the main examination, going through question banks and taking help of my teachers. I was studying at home. To keep myself active, I would go for walks. I had opted for political science in the preliminary and political science and philosophy in the main examination. Since I had both the subjects in BA, I did not have much difficulty in preparing for the main examination. I did not study too many books. I made NCERT books the basis of my preparations. As I was a student of arts, I faced some problems in statistics, but made up for it through sustained practice."

As for the Interview, he says, "It lasted for about 40 minutes and was very cordial. Since I had opted for Hindi medium, so I had no problem in communicating during the interview. The interviewers asked me a lot of questions, including the birthdays of great people. I was asked whose birthday falls on May 3. I was in a dilemma. I told them I did not remember. They still insisted that I try to recollect. I finally replied that I was born on this day. The board members burst out laughing. At that moment, I felt that I would be selected, but did not imagine I would secure 309th rank."

His advice to the candidate appearing for this examination is, "Follow your heart and do what you are interested in. Parents should not force their children to do what they think is best, but guide them so that they can set their aims based on their sphere of interest. The Bollywood movie '3 Idiots' is an excellent example. In the movie, Aamir Khan topped in his class because engineering was not only his interest but also his passion. Students of Hindi medium and those who do not have adequate means can succeed if they plan to become an IAS Officer keeping in mind their interests."

Raise Yourself to Impossible Heights...

This is what IAS topper of 2012, S. Divyadarshini had said, "There is no alternative to hard work. If you wish to pass the IAS examination, then you will have to become obsessive to achieve your objective and work really hard." Divyadarshini, a law graduate from Tamil Nadu's Dr. Ambedkar Law University, had opted for public administration and law as subjects for IAS examination. She prepared both the subjects according to a plan and kept eliminating her weaknesses. Her family members and her mentor Prabhakaran Sir supported her and played a vital role.

Divyadarshini's mother is a housewife and her father is a Customs Consultant. Divyadarshini started preparing immediately after completing her graduation. Her Interview was conducted by Rajni Razdan Board. The Interview went off very well. She says, "I expected to make it, but hadn't really thought that I will top the merit list. To the students who are preparing for this examination, I would say that if you consider yourself capable, success will follow you. Do not be deterred by failure. If you fail, put in twice the effort and maybe you will get success in your last attempt."

Proper Planning Led to Success

This is what Ajay Prakash, who, in the first attempt got 9th rank in the civil services examination, says, "Any objective can be achieved by proper planning. If you have set to join the civil services as your objective and you prepare for it by regular study, there is no reason why you will not succeed."

We talked to him regarding his preparation for this examination and CSAT and this is what he had to say on some of the questions asked:

What is the ideal time for the preparation?

You must start your preparations once you are in the final year of Graduation. Choose your optional subjects. The students get ample time to think. Choose the subjects considering your strengths and weaknesses and follow your heart. It ensures that your self-confidence will be sustained.

Tell us about your educational background?

I belong to Samastipur district in Bihar. I completed my class XII from Bokaro and graduation from Delhi University. Presently, I am doing my M.Phil. from Jawaharlal Nehru

University. Before beginning my preparations for the IAS examination, I wanted to have an alternative option. That is why, after taking admission for the M.Phil course, I appeared for the IAS examination. Candidates preparing for the Civil Services Examination must have at least one alternative career option. If you have an alternative option for your future, then you can prepare in a better manner.

How many hours of study is required for the preparation?

There are no fixed rules. You can study for as long as you are able to. I think that if you study for 4–5 hours regularly, then you can succeed in the examination. To succeed in this examination, do not count the number of hours of study, but study considering the syllabus to be covered.

What were your optional subjects? Which attempt was this? What strategy did you adopt for the preparation?

This was my first attempt. My optional subjects were English Literature and Sociology. I had Sociology in my preliminary examination also. For the preparation, I first selected the best book from the point of view of syllabus coverage and then made a proper plan to study it. I made a one-year plan for all the three examinations and allocated time for all the subjects. If you complete preparation for the main examination ahead of the preliminary examination, then it makes things easier for you.

After the introduction of CSAT, English was made compulsory for the preliminary examination. How should the Hindi medium candidates prepare themselves?

Often it is said that candidates of Hindi medium face problems in the IAS examination. This is not true. Candidates of Hindi medium can speak in Hindi during the interview. The syllabus of English is such that it only tests your understanding of the subject. This minimum knowledge is expected in any service. If your English of class X level is good and you can read and write properly, you will face no problem. This minimum standard of English is definitely expected from an IAS officer, who can be posted in any part of the country.

What is your advice to candidates preparing for this examination?

If you believe in yourself and have the obsession to work hard, then no examination is difficult. Appear for the examination only when you are fully prepared and are completely satisfied with your preparation. If you spot some weaknesses, it will be better if you address them and then appear for the examination. If you appear for the examination after such a preparation and put in the maximum effort in the first attempt, then you are bound to succeed. Although four attempts are allowed, you should consider your first attempt as the last attempt and put in your soul, then one seat will be reserved for you. Do not avoid English. Put in every effort to learn it. Without learning, all languages appear difficult, but after learning them, the same languages become simple.

Success = Studying Continuously

Success is not a commodity found by the roadside. You need to dream and work hard to earn it. This formula fits accurately on Lalit Jain, who, even while facing paucity, cleared the Civil Services examination in the fourth attempt and secured the 41st position. He proved that success in IAS comes after putting in hard work and having an obsession.

Lalit completed his primary education from Saint Jones High School in Sector-26, Kharar, Punjab. He sold newspapers with his father and delivered them from door to door. Some excerpts of the discussion held with Lalit on the IAS examination are reproduced hereunder:

Where did you get the inspiration to join the Civil Service from?

My inspiration came from my grandmother late Vidyavati Jain and maternal grandfather, Deshraj Jain, who was an engineer with the PWD. From a very young age, I always wanted to become an officer. Apart from this, the urge to serve the society further inspired me.

Tell us something about yourself

I completed my class XII with science from DAV. I wasn't interested in engineering. So, I did my B.A. (Honours) in Political Science and secured 75% marks. After it, I got my LLB degree. I was always interested in social service. So I became a student leader. I won more than 100 prizes in debating competitions. Now, I have the IAS platform and through it, I am serving the society in a much better manner.

Whom would you give the credit of your success to?

I will give the credit of my success to my parents, along with the Almighty and then to my friends. If you come from a middle-class family, then your patience is tested all through by this examination. Whenever I lost confidence, the Almighty showed me the way.

Which attempt was this and for how many hours did you study?

Regular study is needed for this examination. I studied for 8–10 hours every day and had fixed the time to study each subject. My subjects were sociology and public administration in the main examination and sociology in the preliminary examination. This was my last attempt. For sociology preparation, I studied NCERT books, IGNOU notes, book by Haralambos, and for public administration, I studied IGNOU notes, Prasad and Prasad, Maheshwari and Awasthi, among others. For general studies, I read all books of NCERT (classes 11 and 12) on all subjects, newspapers, magazines, *Yojna* (planning), NBT Publication's *Bharatiya Samvidhan Va Hamari Sansad* by Subhash Kashyap, among others.

Do you have any message for the aspirants?

Read less, but repeatedly. Work hard and believe in yourself. Have a preparation strategy that suits you. Analyse what you read. Identify weaknesses and rectify them while there is time. Do not be disheartened by financial difficulties but work hard to overcome them. Everyone faces problems and hurdles, but you have the capability to overcome them. If you recognise yourself, then no difficulty can remain permanently.

The story of Gulzar Ahmed Vani

Gulzar Ahmed Vani, 23 years old, who succeeded in the IAS examination in his first attempt, is a resident of Darawa village, in the Vagura region of Baramullah district of Jammu and Kashmir. Baramullah district has been infamous for the bloody battles between the India's defence forces and the militants. Darawa village barely has 100 families and newspapers and magazines are not easily available. Moreover, education facilities are inadequate. In spite of living in such difficult circumstances, Gulzar Ahmed Vani not only dreamt of becoming a civil servant but also fulfilled it in his first attempt. In 2010 UPSC examination, he secured 341st position.

Gulzar Ahmed Vani's father is a small trader. Gulzar Ahmed got his primary education in his village and went to the Jawahar Navodaya Vidyalaya for further studies. It is here that he felt the desire to become a civil servant. Gulzar Ahmed says that many of his friends could not complete their studies and nobody else completed graduation. He says that he was fortunate to have been selected to study at the Jawahar Navoday Vidyalaya, because he got free education and hostel accommodation.

Gulzar Ahmed Vani's goal was set much earlier. In his words, he says, "The educated people in Jammu and Kashmir could not think of anything beyond MBBS or engineering. So I had to convince my father quite a bit for appearing for the Civil Services examination."

He is a Vocal Pedagogy-graduate. He moved to Delhi in 2004. By completing his BA LLB (Honours) from Jamia Milla Islamia University, he was able to fulfil the minimum qualification required to appear for the UPSC examination. He says, "I was confident that one day I will become a civil servant."

Gulzar Ahmed is indebted to a teacher from Kerala who encouraged him to regularly read newspapers and magazines.

For the IAS aspirants, he has this advice: "Do not develop any apprehensions about your preparation. Always remain focussed and keep updating yourself on current affairs through newspapers, magazines and the internet. Develop your analytical skills and try to understand and appreciate all the aspects of an issue. Issues that concern our lives, country or the world are important from the view of UPSC examination. Scientific and technological advancements are also equally important. Also, questions may be asked on medicine and diseases that are causing concern to India and the world. So, develop an approach which will be effective in preparing for the UPSC examination."

❑

10

Come, Let's Practise

With unceasing practice, even a cripple can scale the Himalaya.

—Vedvyasa

PRELIMINARY EXAMINATION – 2022
General Studies Paper-I

1. "Rapid Financing Instrument" and "Rapid Credit Facility" are related to the provisions of lending by which one of the following?
(a) Asian Development Bank
(b) International Monetary Fund
(c) United Nations Environment Programme Finance Initiative
(d) World Bank

2. With reference to the Indian economy, consider the following statements:
1. An increase in Nominal Effective Exchange Rate (NEER) indicates the appreciation of rupee.
2. An increase in the Real Effective Exchange Rate (REER) indicates an improvement in trade competitiveness.
3. An increasing trend in domestic inflation relative to inflation in other countries is likely to cause an increasing divergence between NEER and REER.
Which of the above statements are correct?
(a) 1 and 2 only (b) 2 and 3 only
(c) 1 and 3 only (d) 1, 2 and 3

3. **With reference to the Indian economy, consider the following statements:**
   1. **If the inflation is too high, Reserve Bank of India (RBI) is likely to buy government securities.**
   2. **If the rupée is rapidly depreciating, RBI is likely to sell dollars in the market.**
   3. **If interest rates in the USA or European Union were to fall, that is likely to induce RBI to buy dollars.**

   Which of the statements given above are correct?

   (a) 1 and 2 only (b) 2 and 3 only
   (c) 1 and 3 only (d) 1, 2 and 3

4. **With reference to the "G20 Common Framework", consider the following statements:**
   1. **It is an initiative endorsed by the G20 together with the Paris Club.**
   2. **It is an initiative to support Low Income Countries with unsustainable debt.**

   Which of the statements given above is/are correct?

   (a) 1 only (b) 2 only
   (c) Both 1 and 2 (d) Neither 1 nor 2

5. **With reference to the Indian economy, what are the advantages of "Inflation-Indexed Bonds (IIBs)"?**
   1. **Government can reduce the coupon rates on its borrowing by way of IIBs.**
   2. **IIBs provide protection to the investors from uncertainty regarding inflation.**
   3. **The interest received as well as capital gains on IIBs are not taxable.**

   Which of the statements given above are correct?

   (a) 1 and 2 only (b) 2 and 3 only
   (c) 1 and 3 only (d) 1, 2 and 3

6. **With reference to foreign-owned e-commerce firms operating in India, which of the following statements is/are correct?**
   1. **They can sell their own goods in addition to offering their platforms as market-places.**
   2. **The degree to which they can own big sellers on their platforms is limited.**

Select the correct answer using the code given below:

(a) 1 only
(b) 2 only
(c) Both 1 and 2
(d) Neither 1. nor 2

7. **Which of the following activities constitute real sector in the economy?**
   1. **Farmers harvesting their crops**
   2. **Textile mills converting raw cotton into fabrics**
   3. **A commercial bank lending money to a trading company**
   4. **A corporate body issuing Rupee Denominated Bonds overseas**

   Select the correct answer using the code given below:

   (a) 1 and 2 only
   (b) 2, 3 and 4 only
   (c) 1, 3 and 4 only
   (d) 1, 2, 3 and 4

8. **Which one of the following situations best reflects "Indirect Transfers" often talked about in media recently with reference to India?**

   (a) An Indian company investing in a foreign enterprise and paying taxes to the foreign country on the profits arising out of its investment
   (b) A foreign company investing in India and paying taxes to the country of its base on the profits arising out of its investment
   (c) An Indian company purchases tangible assets in a foreign country and sells such assets after their value increases and transfers the proceeds to India
   (d) A foreign company transfers shares and such shares derive their substantial value from assets located in India

9. **With reference to the expenditure made by an organisation or a company, which of the following statements is/are correct?**
   1. **Acquiring new technology is capital expenditure.**
   2. **Debt financing is considered capital expenditure, while equity financing is considered revenue expenditure.**

Select the correct answer using the code given below :

(a) 1 only (b) 2 only
(c) Both 1 and 2 (d) Neither 1 nor 2

10. With reference to the Indian economy, consider the following statements:

1. A share of the household financial savings goes towards government borrowings.

2. Dated securities issued at market-related rates in auctions form a large component of internal debt.

Which of the above statements is/are correct?

(a) 1 only (b) 2 only
(c) Both 1 and 2 (d) Neither 1 nor 2

11. Consider the following statements:

1. Pursuant to the report of H.N. Sanyal Committee, the Contempt of Courts Act, 1971 was passed.

2. The Constitution of India empowers the Supreme Court and the High Courts to punish for contempt of themselves.

3. The Constitution of India defines Civil Contempt and Criminal Contempt.

4. In India, the Parliament is vested with the powers to make laws on Contempt of Court.

Which of the statements given above is/are correct ?

(a) 1 and 2 only (b) 1, 2 and 4
(c) 3 and 4 only (d) 3 only

12. With reference to India, consider the following statements:

1. Government law officers and legal firms are recognised as advocates, but corporate lawyers and patent attorneys are excluded from recognition as advocates.

2. Bar Councils have the power to lay down the rules relating to legal education and recognition of law colleges.

Which of the statements given above is/are correct?

(a) 1 only (b) 2 only
(c) Both 1 and 2 (d) Neither 1 nor 2

13. Consider the following statements:
    1. A bill amending the Constitution requires a prior recommendation of the President of India.
    2. When a Constitution Amendment Bill is presented to the President of India, it is obligatory for the President of India to give his/her assent.
    3. A Constitution Amendment Bill must be passed by both the Lok Sabha and the Rajya Sabha by a special majority and there is no provision for joint sitting.

    Which of the statements given above are correct?
    (a) 1 and 2 only (b) 2 and 3 only
    (c) 1 and 3 only (d) 1, 2 and 3
14. Consider the following statements:
    1. The Constitution of India classifies the ministers into four ranks viz. Cabinet Minister, Minister of State with Independent Charge, Minister of State and Deputy Minister.
    2. The total number of ministers in the Union Government, including the Prime Minister, shall not exceed 15 percent of the total number of members in the Lok Sabha.

    Which of the statements given above is/are correct?
    (a) 1 only (b) 2 only
    (c) Both 1 and 2 (d) Neither 1 nor 2
15. Which of the following is/are the exclusive power(s) of Lok Sabha ?
    1. To ratify the declaration of Emergency
    2. To pass a motion of no-confidence against the Council of Ministers
    3. To impeach the President of India

    Select the correct answer using the code given below:
    (a) 1 and 2 (b) 2 only
    (c) 1 and 3 (d) 3 only
16. With reference to anti-defection law in India, consider the following statements:
    1. The law specifies that a nominated législator cannot join any political party within six months of being appointed to the House.

2. **The law does not provide any time-frame within which the presiding officer has to decide a defection case.**

Which of the statements given above is/are correct?

(a) 1 only (b) 2 only
(c) Both 1 and 2 (d) Neither 1 nor 2

17. **Consider the following statements:**
    1. **Attorney General of India and Solicitor General of India are the only officers of the Government who are allowed to participate in the meetings of the Parliament of India.**
    2. **According to the Constitution of India, the Attorney General of India submits his resignation when the Government which appointed him resigns.**

    Which of the statements given above is/are correct?

    (a) 1 only (b) 2 only
    (c) Both 1 and 2 (d) Neither 1 nor 2

18. **With reference to the writs issued by the Courts in India, consider the following statements:**
    1. **Mandamus will not lie against a private organisation unless it is entrusted with a public duty.**
    2. **Mandamus will not lie against a Company even though it may be a Government Company.**
    3. **Any public minded person can be a petitioner to move the Court to obtain the writ of Quo Warranto.**

    Which of the statements given above are correct?

    (a) 1 and 2 only (b) 2 and 3 only
    (c) 1 and 3 only (d) 1, 2 and 3

19. **With reference to Ayushman Bharat Digital Mission, consider the following statements:**
    1. **Private and public hospitals must adopt it.**
    2. **As it aims to achieve universal health coverage, every citizen of India should be part of it ultimately.**
    3. **It has seamless portability across the country.**

    Which of the statements given above is/are correct?

    (a) 1 and 2 only (b) 3 only
    (c) 1 and 3 only (d) 1, 2 and 3

20. With reference to Deputy Speaker of Lok Sabha, consider the following statements:

1. As per the Rules of Procedure and Conduct of Business in Lok Sabha, the election of Deputy Speaker shall be held on such date as the Speaker may fix.

2. There is a mandatory provision that the election of a candidate as Deputy Speaker of Lok Sabha shall be from either the principal opposition party or the ruling party.

3. The Deputy Speaker has the same power as of the Speaker when presiding over the sitting of the House and no appeal lies against his rulings.

4. The well established parliamentary practice regarding the appointment of Deputy Speaker is that the motion is moved by the Speaker and duly seconded by the Prime Minister.

Which of the statements given above are correct?

(a) 1 and 3 only (b) 1, 2 and 3
(c) 3 and 4 only (d) 2 and 4 only

21. Among the following crops, which one is the most important anthropogenic source of both methane and nitrous oxide?

(a) Cotton (b) Rice
(c) Sugarcane (d) Wheat

22. "System of Rice Intensification" of cultivation, in which alternate wetting and drying of rice fields is practised, results in:

1. Reduced seed requirement

2. Reduced methane production

3. Reduced electricity consumption

Select the correct answer using the code given below:

(a) 1 and 2 only (b) 2 and 3 only
(c) 1 and 3 only (d) 1, 2 and 3

23. Which one of the following lakes of West Africa has become dry and turned into a desert?

(a) Lake Victoria (b) Lake Faguibine
(c) Lake Oguta (d) Lake Volta

24. Gandikota canyon of South India was created by which one of the following rivers?

(a) Cauvery (b) Manjira

(c) Pennar (d) Tungabhadra

25. Consider the following pairs:

	Peak		*Mountains*
1.	**Namcha Barwa**	**—**	**Garhwal Himalaya**
2.	**Nanda Devi**	**—**	**Kumaon Himalaya**
3.	**Nokrek**	**—**	**Sikkim Himalaya**

Which of the pairs given above is/are correctly matched?

(a) 1 and 2 (b) 2 only

(c) 1 and 3 (d) 3 only

26. The term "Levant" often heard in the news roughly corresponds to which of the following regions?

(a) Region along the eastern Mediterranean shores

(b) Region along North African shores stretching from Egypt to Morocco

(c) Region along Persian Gulf and Horn of Africa

(d) The entire coastal areas of Mediterranean Sea

27. Consider the following countries:

1. Azerbaijan
2. Kyrgyzstan
3. Tajikistan
4. Turkmenistan
5. Uzbekistan

Which of the above have borders with Afghanistan?

(a) 1, 2 and 5 only

(b) 1, 2, 3 and 4 only

(c) 3, 4 and 5 only

(d) 1, 2, 3, 4 and 5

28. With reference to India, consider the following statements:

1. Monazite is a source of rare earths.
2. Monazite contains thorium.
3. Monazite occurs naturally in the entire Indian coastal sands in India.
4. In India, Government bodies only can process or export monazite.

Which of the statements given above are correct?

(a) 1, 2 and 3 only (b) 1, 2 and 4 only
(c) 3 and 4 only (d) 1, 2, 3 and 4

29. In the northern hemisphere, the longest day of the year normally occurs in the:

(a) First half of the month of June
(b) Second half of the month of June
(c) First half of the month of July
(d) Second half of the month of July

30. Consider the following pairs:

	Wetland/Lake		*Location*
1.	**Hokera Wetland**	–	**Punjab**
2.	**Renuka Wetland**	–	**Himachal Pradesh**
3.	**Rudrasagar Lake**	–	**Tripura**
4.	**Sasthamkotta Lake**	–	**Tamil Nadu**

How many pairs given above are correctly matched?

(a) Only one pair (b) Only two pairs
(c) Only three pairs (d) All four pairs

31. Consider the following:

1. Aarogya Setu
2. CoWIN
3. DigiLocker
4. DIKSHA

Which of the above are built on top of open-source digital platforms?

(a) 1 and 2 only (b) 2, 3 and 4 only
(c) 1, 3 and 4 only (d) 1, 2, 3 and 4

32. With reference to Web 3.0, consider the following statements :

1. Web 3.0 technology enables people to control their own data.
2. In Web 3.0 world, there can be blockchain based social networks.
3. Web 3.0 is operated by users collectively rather than a corporation.

Which of the statements given above are correct?

(a) 1 and 2 only (b) 2 and 3 only
(c) 1 and 3 only (d) 1, 2 and 3

33. With reference to "Software as a Service (SaaS)", consider the following statements:

1. SaaS buyers can customise the user interface and can change data fields.

2. SaaS users can access their data through their mobile devices.

3. Outlook, Hotmail and Yahoo! Mail are forms of SaaS.

Which of the statements given above are correct?

(a) 1 and 2 only (b) 2 and 3 only
(c) 1 and 3 only (d) 1, 2 and 3

34. Which one of the following statements best reflects the idea behind the "Fractional Orbital Bombardment System" often talked about in media?

(a) A hypersonic missile is launched into space to counter the asteroid approaching the Earth and explode it in space.
(b) A spacecraft lands on another planet after making several orbital motions.
(c) A missile is put into a stable orbit around the Earth and deorbits over a target on the Earth.
(d) A spacecraft moves along a comet with the same speed and places a probe on its surface.

35. Which one of the following is the context in which the term "qubit" is mentioned?

(a) Cloud Services
(b) Quantum Computing
(c) Visible Light Communication Technologies
(d) Wireless Communication Technologies

36. Consider the following communication technologies :

1. Closed-circuit Television

2. Radio Frequency Identification

3. Wireless Local Area Network

Which of the above are considered Short-Range devices/ technologies?

(a) 1 and 2 only (b) 2 and 3 only
(c) 1 and 3 only (d) 1, 2 and 3

37. **Consider the following statements:**
    1. **Biofilms can form on medical implants within human tissues.**
    2. **Biofilms can form on food and food processing surfaces.**
    3. **Biofilms can exhibit antibiotic resistance.**

    Which of the statements given above are correct?

    (a) 1 and 2 only (b) 2 and 3 only
    (c) 1 and 3 only (d) 1, 2 and 3

38. **Consider the following statements in respect of probiotics :**
    1. **Probiotics are made of both bacteria and yeast.**
    2. **The organisms in probiotics are found in foods we ingest but they do not naturally occur in our gut.**
    3. **Probiotics help in the digestion of milk sugars.**

    Which of the statements given above is/are correct?

    (a) 1 only (b) 2 only
    (c) 1 and 3 (d) 2 and 3

39. **In the context of vaccines manufactured to prevent COVID-19 pandemic, consider the following statements:**
    1. **The Serum Institute of India produced COVID-19 vaccine named Covishield using mRNA platform.**
    2. **Sputnik V vaccine is manufactured using vector based platform.**
    3. **COVAXIN is an inactivated pathogen based vaccine.**

    Which of the statements given above are correct?

    (a) 1 and 2 only (b) 2 and 3 only
    (c) 1 and 3 only (d) 1, 2 and 3

40. **If a major solar storm (solar flare) reaches the Earth, which of the following are the possible effects on the Earth?**
    1. **GPS and navigation systems could fail.**
    2. **Tsunamis could occur at equatorial regions.**
    3. **Power grids could be damaged.**
    4. **Intense auroras could occur over much of the Earth.**
    5. **Forest fires could take place over much of the planet.**

6. Orbits of the satellites could be disturbed.
7. Shortwave radio communication of the aircraft flying over polar regions could be interrupted.

Select the correct answer using the code given below:

(a) 1, 2, 4 and 5 only (b) 2, 3, 5, 6 and 7 only
(c) 1, 3, 4, 6 and 7 only (d) 1, 2, 3, 4, 5, 6 and 7

41. "Climate Action Tracker" which monitors the emission reduction pledges of different countries is a:

(a) Database created by coalition of research organisations.
(b) Wing of "International Panel of Climate Change"
(c) Committee under "United Nations Framework Convention on Climate Change"
(d) Agency promoted and financed by United Nations Environment Programme and World Bank

42. Consider the following statements:

1. "The Climate Group" is an international non-profit organisation that drives climate action by building large networks and runs them.
2. The International Energy Agency in partnership with the Climate Group launched a global initiative "EP100".
3. EP100 brings together leading companies committed to driving innovation in energy efficiency and increasing competitiveness while delivering on emission reduction goals.
4. Some Indian companies are members of EP100.
5. The International Energy Agency is the Secretariat to the "Under2 Coalition".

Which of the statements given above are correct?

(a) 1, 2, 4 and 5 (b) 1, 3 and 4 only
(c) 2, 3 and 5 only (d) 1, 2, 3, 4 and 5

43. "If rainforests and tropical forests are the lungs of the Earth, then surely wetlands function as its kidneys." Which one of the following functions of wetlands best reflects the above statement?

(a) The water cycle in wetlands involves surface runoff, subsoil percolation and evaporation.

(b) Algae form the nutrient base upon which fish, crustaceans, molluscs, birds, reptiles and mammals thrive.
(c) Wetlands play a vital role in maintaining sedimentation balance and soil stabilisation.
(d) Aquatic plants absorb heavy metals and excess nutrients.

44. In the context of WHO Air Quality Guidelines, consider the following statements:

1. The 24-hour mean of $PM_{2.5}$ should not exceed 15 ug/m^3 and annual mean of $PM_{2.5}$ should not exceed 5 µg/m^3.
2. In a year, the highest levels of ozone pollution occur during the periods of inclement weather.
3. PM_{10} can penetrate the lung barrier and enter the bloodstream.
4. Excessive ozone in the air can trigger asthma.

Which of the statements given above are correct?

(a) 1, 3 and 4 (b) 1 and 4 only
(c) 2, 3 and 4 (d) 1 and 2 only

45. With reference to "Gucchi" sometimes mentioned in the news, consider the following statements:

1. It is a fungus.
2. It grows in some Himalayan forest areas.
3. It is commercially cultivated in the Himalayan foothills of north-eastern India.

Which of the statements given above is/are correct?

(a) 1 only (b) 3 only
(c) 1 and 2 (d) 2 and 3

46. With reference to polyethylene terephthalate, the use of which is so widespread in our daily lives, consider the following statements:

1. Its fibres can be blended with wool and cotton fibres to reinforce their properties.
2. Containers made of it can be used to store any alcoholic beverage.
3. Bottles made of it can be recycled into other products.
4. Articles made of it can be easily disposed of by incineration without causing greenhouse gas emissions.

Which of the statements given above are correct?

(a) 1 and 3 (b) 2 and 4
(c) 1 and 4 (d) 2 and 3

47. **Which of the following is not a bird?**

(a) Golden Mahseer (b) Indian Nightjar
(c) Spoonbill (d) White Ibis

48. **Which of the following are nitrogen-fixing plants?**

1. **Alfalfa**
2. **Amaranth**
3. **Chickpea**
4. **Clover**
5. **Purslane (Kulfa)**
6. **Spinach**

Select the correct answer using the code given below:

(a) 1, 3 and 4 only (b) 1, 3, 5 and 6 only
(c) 2, 4, 5 and 6 only (d) 1, 2, 4, 5 and 6

49. **"Biorock technology" is talked about in which one of the following situations?**

(a) Restoration of damaged coral reefs
(b) Development of building materials using plant residues
(c) Identification of areas exploration/extraction of shale gas.
(d) Providing salt licks for wild animals in forests/protected areas

50. **The "Miyawaki method" is well known for the:**

(a) Promotion of commercial farming in arid and semi-arid areas
(b) Development of gardens using genetically modified flora
(c) Creation of mini forests in urban areas
(d) Harvesting wind energy on coastal areas and on sea surfaces

51. **In the Government of India Act 1919, the functions of Provincial Government were divided into "Reserved" and "Transferred" subjects. Which of the following were treated as "Reserved" subjects?**

1. **Administration of Justice**

2. Local Self-Government
3. Land Revenue
4. Police

Select the correct answer using the code given below:

(a) 1, 2 and 3 (b) 2, 3 and 4
(c) 1, 3 and 4 (d) 1, 2 and 4

52. In medieval India, the term "Fanam" referred to:

(a) Clothing (b) Coins
(c) Ornaments (d) Weapons

53. Consider the following freedom fighters:

1. Barindra Kumar Ghosh
2. Jogesh Chandra Chatterjee
3. Rash Behari Bose

Who of the above was/were actively associated with the Ghadar Party?

(a) 1 and 2 (b) 2 only
(c) 1 and 3 (d) 3 only

54. With reference to the proposals of Cripps Mission, consider the following statements:

1. The Constituent Assembly would have members nominated by the Provincial Assemblies as well as the Princely States.
2. Any Province, which is not prepared to accept the new Constitution would have the right to sign a separate agreement with Britain regarding its future status.

Which of the statements given above is/are correct?

(a) 1 only (b) 2 only
(c) Both 1 and 2 (d) Neither 1 nor 2

55. With reference to Indian history, consider the following texts:

1. Nettipakarana
2. Parishishtaparvan
3. Avadanashataka
4. Trishashtilakshana Mahapurana

Which of the above are Jaina texts?

(a) 1, 2 and 3 (b) 2 and 4 only
(c) 1, 3 and 4 (d) 2, 3 and 4

56. With reference to Indian history, consider the following pairs:

	Historical person		*Known as*
1.	**Aryadeva**	**—**	**Jaina scholar**
2.	**Dignaga**	**—**	**Buddhist scholar**
3.	**Nathamuni**	**—**	**Vaishnava scholar**

How many pairs given above are correctly matched ?

(a) None of the pairs (b) Only one pair
(c) Only two pairs (d) All three pairs

57. With reference to Indian history, consider the following statements:

1. The first Mongol invasion of India happened during the reign of Jalal-ud-din Khalji.
2. During the reign of Ala-ud-din Khalji, one Mongol assault marched up to Delhi and besieged the city.
3. Muhammad-bin-Tughlaq temporarily lost portions of north-west of his kingdom to Mongols.

Which of the statements given above is/are correct?

(a) 1 and 2 (b) 2 only
(c) 1 and 3 (d) 3 only

58. With reference to Indian history, who of the following were known as "Kulah-Daran"?

(a) Arab merchants (b) Qalandars
(c) Persian calligraphists (d) Sayyids

59. With reference to Indian history, consider the following statements:

1. The Dutch established their factories/warehouses on the east coast on lands granted to them by Gajapati rulers.
2. Alfonso de Albuquerque captured Goa from the Bijapur Sultanate.
3. The English East India Company established a factory at Madras on a plot of land leased from a representative of the Vijayanagara empire.

Which of the statements given above are correct?

(a) 1 and 2 only (b) 2 and 3 only
(c) 1 and 3 only (d) 1, 2 and 3

60. According to Kautilya's Arthashastra, which of the following are correct?

1. A person could be a slave as a result of a judicial punishment.

2. If a female slave bore her master a son, she was legally free.

3. If a son born to a female slave was fathered by her master, the son was entitled to the legal status of the master's son.

Which of the statements given above are correct?

(a) 1 and 2 only (b) 2 and 3 only
(c) 1 and 3 only (d) 1, 2 and 3

61. Consider the following statements :

1. Tight monetary policy of US Federal Reserve could lead to capital flight.

2. Capital flight may increase the interest cost of firms with existing External Commercial Borrowings (ECBs).

3. Devaluation of domestic currency decreases the currency risk associated with ECBS.

Which of the statements given above are correct?

(a) 1 and 2 only (b) 2 and 3 only
(c) 1 and 3 only (d) 1, 2 and 3

62. Consider the following States:

1. Andhra Pradesh

2. Kerala

3. Himachal Pradesh

4. Tripura

How many of the above are generally known as tea-producing States?

(a) Only one State (b) Only two States
(c) Only three States (d) All four States

63. Consider the following statements:

1. In India, credit rating agencies are regulated by Reserve Bank of India.

2. The rating agency popularly known as ICRA is a public limited company.

3. **Brickwork Ratings is an Indian credit rating agency.**

Which of the statements given above are correct?

(a) 1 and 2 only (b) 2 and 3 only
(c) 1 and 3 only (d) 1, 2 and 3

64. With reference to the 'Banks Board Bureau (BBB)', which of the following statements are correct?

1. **The Governor of RBI is the Chairman of BBB.**
2. **BBB recommends for the selection of heads for Public Sector Banks.**
3. **BBB helps the Public Sector Banks in developing strategies and capital raising plans.**

Select the correct answer using the code given below:

(a) 1 and 2 only (b) 2 and 3 only
(c) 1 and 3 only (d) 1, 2 and 3

65. With reference to Convertible Bonds, consider the following statements:

1. **As there is an option to exchange the bond for equity, Convertible Bonds pay a lower rate of interest.**
2. **The option to convert to equity affords the bondholder a degree of indexation to rising consumer prices.**

Which of the statements given above is/are correct?

(a) 1 only (b) 2 only
(c) Both 1 and 2 (d) Neither 1 nor 2

66. Consider the following:

1. **Asian Infrastructure Investment Bank**
2. **Missile Technology Control Regime**
3. **Shanghai Cooperation Organisation**

India is a member of which of the above?

(a) 1 and 2 only (b) 3 only
(c) 2 and 3 only (d) 1, 2 and 3

67. Consider the following statements:

1. **Vietnam has been one of the fastest growing economies in the world in the recent years.**
2. **Vietnam is led by a multi-party political system.**

3. **Vietnam's economic growth is linked to its integration with global supply chains and focus on exports.**
4. **For a long time Vietnam's low labour costs and stable exchange rates have attracted global manufacturers.**
5. **Vietnam has the most productive e-service sector in the Indo-Pacific region.**

Which of the statements given above are correct?

(a) 2 and 4 (b) 3 and 5
(c) 1, 3 and 4 (d) 1 and 2

68. In India, which one of the following is responsible for maintaining price stability by controlling inflation?

(a) Department of Consumer Affairs
(b) Expenditure Management Commission
(c) Financial Stability and Development Council
(d) Reserve Bank of India

69. With reference to Non-Fungible Tokens (NFTs), consider the following statements:

1. **They enable the digital representation of physical assets.**
2. **They are unique cryptographic tokens that exist on a blockchain.**
3. **They can be traded or exchanged at equivalency and therefore can be used as a medium of commercial transactions.**

Which of the statements given above are correct?

(a) 1 and 2 only (b) 2 and 3 only
(c) 1 and 3 only (d) 1, 2 and 3

70. Consider the following pairs:

	Reservoirs		*States*
1.	**Ghataprabha**	—	**Telangana**
2.	**Gandhi Sagar**	—	**Madhya Pradesh**
3.	**Indira Sagar**	—	**Andhra Pradesh**
4.	**Maithon**	—	**Chhattisgarh**

How many pairs given above are not correctly matched?

(a) Only one pair (b) Only two pairs
(c) Only three pairs (d) All four pairs

71. In India, which one of the following compiles information on industrial disputes, closures, retrenchments and lay-offs in factories employing workers?

(a) Central Statistics Office
(b) Department for Promotion of Industry and Internal Trade
(c) Labour Bureau
(d) National Technical Manpower Information System

72. In India, what is the role of the Coal Controller's Organisation (CCO)?

1. CCO is the major source of Coal Statistics in Government of India.
2. It monitors progress of development of Captive Coal/Lignite blocks.
3. It hears any objection to the Government's notification relating to acquisition of coal-bearing areas.
4. It ensures that coal mining companies deliver the coal to end users in the prescribed time.

Select the correct answer using the code given below:

(a) 1, 2 and 3 (b) 3 and 4 only
(c) 1 and 2 only (d) 1, 2 and 4

73. If a particular area is brought under the Fifth Schedule of the Constitution of India, which one of the following statements best reflects the consequence of it?

(a) This would prevent the transfer of land of tribal people to non-tribal people.
(b) This would create a local self-governing body in that area.
(c) This would convert that area into a Union Territory.
(d) The State having such areas would be declared a Special Category State.

74. Consider the following statements:

1. The India Sanitation Coalition is a platform to promote sustainable sanitation and is funded by the Government of India and the World Health Organisation.

2. **The National Institute of Urban Affairs is an apex body of the Ministry of Housing and Urban Affairs in Government of India and provides innovative solutions to address the challenges of Urban India.**

Which of the statements given above is/are correct?

(a) 1 only (b) 2 only
(c) Both 1 and 2 (d) Neither 1 nor 2

75. **Which one of the following has been constituted under the Environment (Protection) Act, 1986 ?**
(a) Central Water Commission
(b) Central Ground Water Board
(c) Central Ground Water Authority
(d) National Water Development Agency

76. **With reference to the "United Nations Credentials Committee", consider the following statements:**
1. **It is a committee set up by the UN Security Council and works under its supervision.**
2. **It traditionally meets in March, June and September every year.**
3. **It assesses the credentials of all UN members before submitting a report to the General Assembly for approval.**

Which of the statements given above is/are correct?

(a) 3 only (b) 1 and 3
(c) 2 and 3 (d) 1 and 2

77. **Which one of the following statements best describes the 'Polar Code'?**
(a) It is the international code of safety for ships operating in polar waters.
(b) It is the agreement of the countries around the North Pole regarding the demarcation of their territories in the polar region.
(c) It is a set of norms to be followed by the countries whose scientists undertake research studies in the North Pole and South Pole.
(d) It is a trade and security agreement of the member countries of the Arctic Council.

78. With reference to the United Nations General Assembly, consider the following statements:

1. The UN General Assembly can grant observer status to the non-member States.

2. Inter-governmental organisations can seek observer status in the UN General Assembly.

3. Permanent Observers in the UN General Assembly can maintain missions at the UN headquarters.

Which of the statements given above are correct?

(a) 1 and 2 only (b) 2 and 3 only
(c) 1 and 3 only (d) 1, 2 and 3

79. With reference to the "Tea Board" in India, consider the following statements:

1. The Tea Board is a statutory body.

2. It is a regulatory body attached to the Ministry of Agriculture and Farmers Welfare.

3. The Tea Board's Head Office is situated in Bengaluru.

4. The Board has overseas offices at Dubai and Moscow.

Which of the statements given above are correct?

(a) 1 and 3 (b) 2 and 4
(c) 3 and 4 (d) 1 and 4

80. Which one of the following best describes the term "greenwashing"?

(a) Conveying a false impression that a company's products are eco-friendly and environmentally sound

(b) Non-inclusion of ecological/environmental costs in the Annual Financial Statements of a country

(c) Ignoring the disastrous ecological consequences while undertaking infrastructure development

(d) Making mandatory provisions for environmental costs in a government project/programme

81. Consider the following statements:

1. High clouds primarily reflect solar radiation and cool the surface of the Earth.

2. Low clouds have a high absorption of infrared radiation emanating from the Earth's surface and thus cause warming effect.

Which of the statements given above is/are correct?

(a) 1 only (b) 2 only
(c) Both 1 and 2 (d) Neither 1 nor 2

82. Consider the following statements:

1. **Bidibidi is a large refugee settlement in north-western Kenya.**
2. **Some people who fled from South Sudan civil war live in Bidibidi.**
3. **Some people who fled from civil war in Somalia live in Dadaab refugee complex in Kenya.**

Which of the statements given above is/are correct?

(a) 1 and 2 (b) 2 only
(c) 2 and 3 (d) 3 only

83. Consider the following countries:

1. **Armenia**
2. **Azerbaijan**
3. **Croatia**
4. **Romania**
5. **Uzbekistan**

Which of the above are members of the Organisation of Turkic States?

(a) 1, 2 and 4 (b) 1 and 3
(c) 2 and 5 (d) 3, 4 and 5

84. Consider the following statements:

1. **Gujarat has the largest solar park in India.**
2. **Kerala has a fully solar powered International Airport.**
3. **Goa has the largest floating solar photovoltaic project in India.**

Which of the statements given above is/are correct?

(a) 1 and 2 (b) 2 only
(c) 1 and 3 (d) 3 only

85. With reference to to the United Nations Convention on the Law of Sea, consider the following statements:

1. **A coastal state has the right to establish the breadth of its territorial sea up to a limit not exceeding 12**

nautical miles, measured from baseline determined in accordance with the convention.

2. **Ships of all states, whether coastal or land-locked, enjoy the right of innocent passage through the territorial sea.**
3. **The Exclusive Economic Zone shall not extend beyond 200 nautical miles from the baseline from which the breadth of the territorial sea is measured.**

Which of the statements given above are correct?

(a) 1 and 2 only (b) 2 and 3 only
(c) 1 and 3 only (d) 1, 2 and 3

86. **Which one of the following statements best reflects the issue with Senkaku Islands, sometimes mentioned in the news?**
    (a) It is generally believed that they are artificial islands made by a country around South China Sea.
    (b) China and Japan engage in maritime disputes over these islands in East China Sea.
    (c) A permanent American military base has been set up there to help Taiwan to increase its defence capabilities.
    (d) Though International Court of Justice declared them as no man's land, some South-East Asian countries claim them.

87. **Consider the following pairs:**

	Country		*Important reason for being in the news recently*
1.	**Chad**	–	**Setting up of permanent military base by China**
2.	**Guinea**	–	**Suspension of Constitution and Government by military**
3.	**Lebanon**	–	**Severe and prolonged economic depression**
4.	**Tunisia**	–	**Suspension of Parliament by President**

How many pairs given above are correctly matched?

(a) Only one pair (b) Only two pairs
(c) Only three pairs (d) All four pairs

88. Consider the following pairs:

	Region often mentioned in the news		*Country*
1.	**Anatolia**	–	**Turkey**
2.	**Amhara**	–	**Ethiopia**
3.	**Cabo Delgado**	–	**Spain**
4.	**Catalonia**	–	**Italy**

How many pairs given above are correctly matched?

(a) Only one pair (b) Only two pairs
(c) Only three pairs (d) All four pairs

89. With reference to Indian laws about wildlife protection, consider the following statements:

1. Wild animals are the sole property of the government.

2. When a wild animal is declared protected, such animal is entitled for equal protection whether it is found in protected areas or outside.

3. Apprehension of a protected wild animal becoming a danger to human life is sufficient ground for its capture or killing.

Which of the statements given above is/are correct?

(a) 1 and 2 (b) 2 only
(c) 1 and 3 (d) 3 only

90. Certain species of which one of the following organisms are well known as cultivators of fungi?

(a) Ant (b) Cockroach
(c) Crab (d) Spider

91. Consider the following pairs:

	Site of Ashoka's major rock edicts		*Location in the State of*
1.	**Dhauli**	–	**Odisha**
2.	**Erragudi**	–	**Andhra Pradesh**
3.	**Jaugada**	–	**Madhya Pradesh**
4.	**Kalsi**	–	**Karnataka**

How many pairs given above are correctly matched?

(a) Only one pair (b) Only two pairs
(c) Only three pairs (d) All four pairs

92. Consider the following pairs:

	King		*Dynasty*
1.	**Nannuka**	**–**	**Chandela**
2.	**Jayashakti**	**–**	**Paramara**
3.	**Nagabhata II**	**–**	**Gurjara-Pratihara**
4.	**Bhoja**	**–**	**Rashtrakuta**

How many pairs given above are correctly matched?

(a) Only one pair
(b) Only two pairs
(c) Only three pairs
(d) All four pairs

93. Which one of the following statements about Sangam literature in ancient South India is correct?

(a) Sangam poems are devoid of any reference to material culture.
(b) The social classification of Varna was known to Sangam poets.
(c) Sangam poems have no reference to warrior ethic.
(d) Sangam literature refers to magical forces as irrational.

94. "Yogavasistha" was translated into Persian by Nizamuddin Panipati during the reign of:

(a) Akbar
(b) Humayun
(c) Shahjahan
(d) Aurangzeb

95. The world's second tallest statue in sitting pose of Ramanuja was inaugurated by the Prime Minister of India at Hyderabad recently. Which one of the following statements correctly represents the teachings of Ramanuja?

(a) The best means of salvation was devotion.
(b) Vedas are eternal, self-existent and wholly authoritative.
(c) Logical arguments were essential means for the highest bliss.
(d) Salvation was to be obtained through meditation.

96. The Prime Minister recently inaugurated the new Circuit House near Somnath Temple at Veraval. Which

of the following statements are correct regarding Somnath Temple?

1. **Somnath Temple is one of the Jyotirlinga shrines.**
2. **A description of Somnath Temple was given by Al-Biruni.**
3. **Pran Pratishtha of Somnath Temple (installation of the present day temple) was done by President S. Radhakrishnan.**

Select the correct answer using the code given below :

(a) 1 and 2 only
(b) 2 and 3 only
(c) 1 and 3 only
(d) 1, 2 and 3

97. Which one of the following statements best describes the role of B cells and T cells in the human body?

(a) They protect the body from environmental allergens.
(b) They alleviate the body's pain and inflammation.
(c) They act as immunosuppressants in the body.
(d) They protect the body from the diseases caused by pathogens.

98. Consider the following statements:

1. **Other than those made by humans, nanoparticles do not exist in nature.**
2. **Nanoparticles of some metallic oxides are used in the manufacture of some cosmetics.**
3. **Nanoparticles of some commercial products which enter the environment are unsafe for humans.**

Which of the statements given above is/are correct?

(a) 1 only (b) 3 only
(c) 1 and 2 (d) 2 and 3

99. Consider the following statements:

DNA Barcoding can be a tool to:

1. **assess the age of a plant or animal.**
2. **distinguish among species that look alike.**
3. **identify undesirable animal or plant materials in processed foods.**

Which of the statements given above is/are correct?

(a) 1 only (b) 3 only

(c) 1 and 2 (d) 2 and 3

100. Consider the following:

1. Carbon monoxide

2. Nitrogen oxide

3. Ozone

4. Sulphur dioxide

Excess of which of the above in the environment is/are cause(s) of acid rain?

(a) 1, 2 and 3 (b) 2 and 4 only

(c) 4 only (d) 1, 3 and 4

Answers

1. (b) **2.** (c) **3.** (b) **4.** (c) **5.** (a) **6.** (b) **7.** (a) **8.** (d)
9. (a) **10.** (c) **11.** (b) **12.** (b) **13.** (b) **14.** (b) **15.** (b) **16.** (b)
17. (d) **18.** (c) **19.** (b) **20.** (a) **21.** (b) **22.** (d) **23.** (b) **24.** (c)
25. (b) **26.** (a) **27.** (c) **28.** (b) **29.** (b) **30.** (b) **31.** (d) **32.** (d)
33. (d) **34.** (c) **35.** (b) **36.** (d) **37.** (d) **38.** (c) **39.** (b) **40.** (c)
41. (a) **42.** (b) **43.** (d) **44.** (b) **45.** (c) **46.** (a) **47.** (a) **48.**(a)
49. (a) **50.** (c) **51.** (c) **52.** (a) **53.** (d) **54.** (b) **55.** (b) **56.** (c)
57. (b) **58.** (d) **59.** (b) **60.** (d) **61.** (a) **62.** (c) **63.** (b) **64.** (b)
65. (c) **66.** (d) **67.** (c) **68.** (d) **69.** (a) **70.** (c) **71.** (a) **72.** (a)
73. (b) **74.** (b) **75.** (c) **76.** (a) **77.** (a) **78.** (d) **79.** (d) **80.** (a)
81. (d) **82.** (c) **83.** (c) **84.** (b) **85.** (d) **86.** (b) **87.** (c) **88.** (b)
89. (a) **90.** (a) **91.** (b) **92.** (b) **93.** (b) **94.** (a) **95.** (a) **96.** (a)
97. (d) **98.** (d) **99.** (d) **100.** (b)

PRELIMINARY EXAMINATION – 2022
General Studies Paper-II

Directions for the following 3 (three) items:

Read the following two passages and answer the items that follow the passages. Your answers to these items should be based on the passages only.

Passage – 1

The main threat to maintaining progress in human development comes from the increasingly evident unsustainability of production and consumption patterns. Current production models rely heavily on fossil fuels. We now know that this is unsustainable because the resources are finite. The close link between economic growth and greenhouse gas emissions needs to be severed for human development to become truly sustainable. Some developed countries have begun to alleviate the worst effects by expanding recycling and investing in public transport and infrastructure. But most developing countries are hampered by the high costs and low availability of clean energy sources. Developed countries need to support developing countries' transition to sustainable human development.

1. Unsustainability in production pattern is due to which of the following?

1. Heavy dependence on fossil fuels

2. Limited availability of resources

3. Expansion of recycling

Select the correct answer using the code given below.

(a) 1 and 2 only (b) 2 only

(c) 1 and 3 only (d) 1, 2 and 3

2. Consider the following statements:

Developed countries can support developing countries' transition to sustainable human development by

1. making clean energy sources available at low cost

2. providing loans for improving their public transport at nominal interest rates

3. encouraging them to change their production and consumption patterns

Which of the statements given above is/are correct?

(a) 1 only (b) 1 and 2 only
(c) 2 and 3 only (d) 1, 2 and 3

Passage—2

Unless the forces and tendencies which are responsible for destroying the country's environment are checked in the near future and afforestation of denuded areas is taken up on a massive scale, the harshness of the climatic conditions and soil erosion by wind and water will increase to such an extent that agriculture, which is the mainstay of our people, will gradually become impossible. The desert countries of the world and our own desert areas in Rajasthan are a grim reminder of the consequences of large-scale deforestation. Pockets of desert-like landscape are now appearing in other parts of the country including the Sutlej-Ganga Plains and the Deccan Plateau. Where only a few decades back there used to be lush green forests with perennial streams and springs, there is only brown earth, bare of vegetation, without any water in the streams and springs except in the rainy season.

3. **According to the passage given above, deforestation and denudation will ultimately lead to which of the following?**
   1. **Depletion of soil resource**
   2. **Shortage of land for the common man**
   3. **Lack of water for cultivation**

   Select the correct answer using the code given below.

   (a) 1 and 2 only (b) 2 and 3 only
   (c) 1 and 3 only (d) 1, 2 and 3
4. **What is the value of X in the sequence 20, 10, 10, 15, 30, 75, X?**

   (a) 105 (b) 120
   (c) 150 (d) 225
5. **An Identity Card has the number ABCDEFG, not necessarily in that order, where each letter represents a distinct digit (1, 2, 4, 5, 7, 8, 9 only). The number is divisible by 9. After deleting the first digit from the right, the resulting number is divisible by 6. After**

deleting two digits from the right of original number, the resulting number is divisible by 5. After deleting three digits from the right of original number, the resulting number is divisible by 4. After deleting four digits from the right of original number, the resulting number is divisible by 3. After deleting five digits from the right of original number, the resulting number is divisible by 2. Which of the following is a possible value for the sum of the middle three digits of the number?

(a) 8 (b) 9
(c) 11 (d) 12

6. **Two friends X and Y start running and they run together for 50 m in the same direction and reach a point. X turns right and runs 60 m, while Y turns left and runs 40 m. Then X turns left and runs 50 m and stops, while Y turns right and runs 50 m and then stops. How far are the two friends from each other now?**

(a) 100 m (b) 90 m
(c) 60 m (d) 50 m

7. **Which date of June 2099 among the following is Sunday?**

(a) 4 (b) 5
(c) 6 (d) 7

8. **A bill for ₹ 1,840 is paid in the denominations of ₹ 50, ₹ 20 and ₹ 10 notes. ₹ 50 notes in all are used. Consider the following statements:**
   1. **25 notes of ₹50 are used and the remaining are in the denominations of ₹20 and ₹10.**
   2. **35 notes of ₹20 are used and the remaining are in the denominations of ₹50 and ₹10.**
   3. **20 notes of ₹10 are used and the remaining are in the denominations of ₹50 and ₹20.**

Which of the above statements are not correct?

(a) 1 and 2 only (b) 2 and 3 only
(c) 1 and 3 only. (d) 1, 2 and 3

9. **Which number amongst 2^{40}, 3^{21}, 4^{18} and 8^{12} is the smallest?**

(a) 2^{40} (b) 3^{21}
(c) 4^{18} (d) 8^{12}

10. The digits 1 to 9 are arranged in three rows in such a way that each row contains three digits, and the number formed in the second row is twice the number formed in the first row; and the number formed in the third row is thrice the number formed in the first row. Repetition of digits is not allowed. If only three of the four digits 2, 3, 7 and 9 are allowed to use in the first row, how many such combinations are possible to be arranged in the three rows?

(a) 4 (b) 3

(c) 2 (d) 1

Directions for the following 4 (four) items:

Read the following two passages and answer the items that follow the passages. Your answers to these items should be based on the passages only.

Passage – 1

"In simple matters like shoe-making, we think only a specially trained person will serve our purpose, but in politics, we presume that everyone who knows how to get votes knows how to administer a State. When we are ill, we call for a trained physician, whose degree is a guarantee of specific preparation and technical competence – we do not ask for the handsomest physician, or the most eloquent one; well then, when the whole State is ill should we not look for the service and guidance of the wisest and the best?"

11. Which one of the following statements best reflects the message of the author of the passage?

(a) We assume that in a democracy, any politician is qualified to administer a State.

(b) Politicians should be selected from those trained in administration.

(c) We need to devise a method of barring incompetence from public office.

(d) As voters select their administrators, the eligibility of politicians to administer a State cannot be questioned.

Passage—2

The poverty line is quite unsatisfactory when it comes to grasping the extent of poverty in India. It is not only because of its extremely narrow definition of 'who is poor' and the debatable methodology used to count the poor, but also because of a more fundamental assumption underlying it. It exclusively relies on the notion of poverty as insufficient income or insufficient purchasing power. One can better categorise it by calling it income poverty. If poverty is ultimately about deprivations affecting human well-being, then income poverty is only one aspect of it. Poverty of a life, in our view, lies not merely in the impoverished state in which the person actually lives, but also in the lack of real opportunity given by social constraints as well as personal circumstances—to choose other types of living. Even the relevance of low incomes, meagre possessions, and other aspects of what are standardly seen as economic poverty relate ultimately to their role in curtailing capabilities, i.e., their role in severely restricting the choices people have to lead variable and valued lives.

12. Why is the methodology adopted in India to count the 'poor' debatable?

(a) There is some confusion regarding what should constitute the 'poverty line'.

(b) There are wide diversities in the condition of the rural and urban poor.

(c) There is no uniform global standard for measuring income poverty.

(d) It is based on the proposition of poverty as meagre income or buying capacity.

13. Why is income poverty only one measure of counting the 'poor' ?

(a) It talks of only one kind of deprivation ignoring all others.

(b) Other deprivations in a human life have nothing to do with lack of purchasing power.

(c) Income poverty is not a permanent condition, it changes from time to time.

(d) Income poverty restricts human choices only at a point of time.

14. **What does the author mean by 'poverty of a life'?**
    (a) All deprivations in a human life which stem not only from lack of income but lack of real opportunities.
    (b) Impoverished state of poor people in rural and urban areas
    (c) Missed opportunities in diverse personal circumstances
    (d) Material as well as non-material deprivations in a human life which restrict human choices permanently
15. **X and Y run a 3 km race along a circular course of length 300 m. Their speeds are in the ratio 3:2. If they start together in the same direction, how many times would the first one pass the other (the start-off is not counted as passing)?**
    (a) 2 (b) 3
    (c) 4 (d) 5
16. **If the order of the letters in the English alphabet is reversed and each letter represents the letter whose position it occupies, then which one of the following represents 'LUCKNOW'?**
    (a) OGXPMLD (b) OGXQMLE
    (c) OFXPMLE (d) OFXPMLD
17. **In a tournament of Chess having 150 entrants, a player is eliminated whenever he loses a match. It is given that no match results in a tie/draw. How many matches are played in the entire tournament?**
    (a) 151 (b) 150
    (c) 149 (d) 148
18. **How many 3-digit natural numbers (without repetition of digits) are there such that each digit is odd and the number is divisible by 5?**
    (a) 8 (b) 12
    (c) 16 (d) 24
19. **Consider the Question and two Statements given below:**
    Question: Is x an integer?
    Statement-1: x/3 is not an integer.
    Statement-2: 3x is an integer.

Which one of the following is correct in respect of the Question and the Statements?

(a) Statement-1 alone is sufficient to answer the Question
(b) Statement-2 alone is sufficient to answer the Question
(c) Both Statement-1 and Statement-2 are sufficient to answer the Question
(d) Both Statement-1 and Statement-2 are not sufficient to answer the Question

20. The increase in the price of a certain item was 25%. Then the price was decreased by 20% and then again increased by 10%. What is the resultant increase in the price?

(a) 5% (b) 10%
(c) 12.5% (d) 15%

Directions for the following 3 (three) items:

Read the following passage and answer the items that follow the passage. Your answers to these items should be based on the passage only.

Passage

In some places in the world, the productivity of staples such as rice and wheat has reached a plateau. Neither new strains nor fancy agrochemicals are raising the yields. Nor is there much unfarmed land left that is suitable to be brought under the plough. If global temperature continues to rise, some places will become unsuitable for farming. Application of technology can help overcome these problems. Agricultural technology is changing fast. Much of this change is brought about by affluent farmers in the West/Americas. Techniques developed in the West are being adapted in some places to make tropical crops more productive. Technology is of little use if it is not adapted. In the developing world, that applies as much to existing farming techniques as it does to the latest advances in genetic modification. Extending to the smallholders and subsistence farmers of Africa and Asia the best of today's agricultural practices, in such simple matters as how much fertilizers to apply and when, would lead to a greatly increased availability of food for humanity. So would things like better roads and storage facilities, to allow for the carriage of surpluses to markets and reduce wastage.

21. Based on the above passage, the following assumptions have been made:

1. Development of agricultural technology is confined to developed countries.

2. Agricultural technology is not adapted in developing countries.

Which of the above assumptions is/are valid?

(a) 1 only (b) 2 only
(c) Both 1 and 2 (d) Neither 1 nor 2

22. Based on the above passage, following assumptions have been made:

1. Poor countries need to bring about change in their existing farming techniques.

2. Developed countries have better infrastructure and they waste less food.

Which of the above assumptions is/are valid?

(a) 1 only (b) 2 only
(c) Both 1 and 2 (d) Neither 1 nor 2

23. Based on the above passage, the following assumptions have been made:

1. Growing enough food for future generations will be a challenge.

2. Corporate farming is a viable option for food security in poor countries.

Which of the above assumptions is/are valid?

(a) I only (b) 2 only
(c) Both 1 and 2 (d) Neither 1 nor 2

24. The letters A, B, C, D and E are arranged in such a way that there are exactly two letters between A and E. How many such arrangements are possible?

(a) 12 (b) 18
(c) 24 (d) 36

25. Consider the Question and two Statements given below:

Question: Is Z brother of X?

Statement-1: X is a brother of Y and Y is a brother of Z.
Statement-2: X, Y and Z are siblings.
Which one of the following is correct in respect of the Question and the Statements?

(a) Statement-1 alone is sufficient to answer the Question
(b) Statement-2 alone is sufficient to answer the Question
(c) Both Statement-1 and Statement-2 are sufficient to answer the Question
(d) Both Statement-1 and Statement-2 are not sufficient to answer the Question

26. On one side of a 1.01 km long road, 101 plants are planted at equal distance from each other. What is the total distance between 5 consecutive plants?

(a) 40.4 m (b) 40 m
(c) 50 m (d) 50.5 m

27. A, B and C are three places such that there are three different roads from A to B, four different roads from B to C and three different roads from A to C. In how many different ways can one travel from A to C using these roads?

(a) 10 (b) 13
(c) 15 (d) 36

28. A has some coins. He gives half of the coins and 2 more to B. B gives half of the coins and 2 more to C. C gives half of the coins and 2 more to D. The number of coins D has now, is the smallest two-digit number. How many coins does A have in the beginning?

(a) 76 (b) 68
(c) 60 (d) 52

29. In the series AABABCABCDABCDE..., which letter appears at the 100th place?

(a) G (b) H
(c) I (d) J

30. Three persons A, B and C are standing in a queue not necessarily in the same order. There are 4 persons between A and B, and 7 persons between B and C. If

there are 11 persons ahead of C and 13 behind A, what could be the minimum number of persons in the queue?

(a) 22 (b) 28

(c) 32 (d) 38

Directions for the following 4 (four) items:

Read the following two passages and answer the items that follow the passages. Your answers to these items should be based on the passages only.

Passage—1

Natural selection cannot anticipate future environments on the earth. Therefore, the set of existing organisms can never be fully prepared for environmental catastrophes that await life. An outcome of this is the extinction of those species which cannot overcome environmental adversity. This failure to survive, in modern terms, can be attributed to the genomes which are unable to withstand geological vagaries or biological mishaps (infections, diseases and so on). In biological evolution on the earth, extinction of species has been a major feature. The earth may presently have up to ten million species, yet more than 90% of species that have ever lived on the earth are now extinct. Once again, the creationist doctrines fail to satisfactorily address why a divine creator will firstly bother to create millions of species and then allow them to perish. The Darwinian explanation for extinct life is once again simple, elegant and at once convincing—organisms go extinct as a function of environmental or biological assaults for which their inheritance deems them ill-equipped. Therefore, the so-called Darwinian theory of evolution is not a theory at all. Evolution happens—this is a fact. The mechanism of evolution (Darwin proposed natural selection) is amply supported by scientific data. Indeed, to date no single zoological, botanical, geological, paleontological, genetic or physical evidence has refuted either of the central two main Darwinian ideas. If religion is not taken into consideration, Darwinian laws are acceptable just like the laws proposed by Copernicus, Galileo, Newton and Einstein—sets of natural laws that explain natural phenomena in the universe.

31. According to to the passage, natural selection cannot anticipate future environments on the earth as

1. species not fully prepared to face the environmental changes that await them will face extinction

2. all the existing species would get extinct as their genomes will not withstand biological mishaps

3. inability of the genome to withstand environmental changes would result in extinction

4. extinction of species is a common feature

Select the correct answer using the code given below.

(a) 1, 2 and 3 (b) 2, 3 and 4
(c) 1, 3 and 4 (d) 1, 2 and 4

32. The passage suggests that Darwinian theory of evolution is not a theory at all because

(a) it does not satisfy the creationist doctrine
(b) extinction is a function of environment and biological assaults
(c) there are no evidences to refute it
(d) existence of organisms is attributed to a creator

33. With reference to the passage, the following assumptions have been made:

1. Only species that have the ability to overcome environmental catastrophes will survive and perpetuate.

2. More than 90% of the species on the earth are in the danger of getting extinct due to drastic changes in the environment.

3. Darwin's theory explains all the natural phenomena.

Which of the above assumptions is/are valid?

(a) 1 only (b) 1 and 2 only
(c) 3 only (d) 1, 2 and 3

Passage – 2

With steady economic growth, higher literacy and increasing skill levels, the number of Indian middle-class families has gone up exponentially. Direct results of the affluence have been changes in dietary patterns and energy consumption levels. People have moved to a higher protein-based diet like milk products, fish and meat, all of which need significantly more water to produce than cereal-based diets. Increasing use of electronic and electric machines/gadgets and motor vehicles needs more and more energy and generation of energy needs water.

34. **Which one of the following statements best reflects the crux of the passage?**
    (a) People should be persuaded to continue with the mainly Indian traditional cereal-based diets.
    (b) India needs to focus on developing agricultural productivity and capacity for more energy generation in the coming years.
    (c) Modern technological developments result in the change of cultural and social behaviour of the people.
    (d) Water management practices in India need to change dramatically in the coming years.

35. **How many seconds in total are there in x weeks, x days, x hours, x minutes and x seconds?**
    (a) 11580x (b) 11581x
    (c) 694860x (d) 694861x

36. **P, Q, R, S, T and U are six members of a family. R is the spouse of Q. U is the mother of T and S is the daughter of U. P's daughter is T and R's son is P. There are two couples in the family. Which one of the following is correct?**
    (a) Q is the grandfather of T
    (b) Q is the grandmother of T
    (c) R is the mother of P
    (d) T is the granddaughter of Q

37. **Consider the Question and two Statements given below in respect of three cities P, Q and R in a State:**
    Question: How far is city P from city Q?
    Statement-1: City Q is 18 km from city R.
    Statement-2: City P is 43 km from city R.
    Which one of the following is correct in respect of the Question and the Statements?

(a) Statement-1 alone is sufficient to answer the Question
(b) Statement-2 alone is sufficient to answer the Question
(c) Both Statement-1 and Statement-2 are sufficient to answer the Question
(d) Both Statement-1 and Statement-2 are not sufficient to answer the Question

38. Two Statements followed by four Conclusions are given below. You have to take the Statements to be true even if they seem to be at variance from the commonly known facts. Read all the Conclusions and then decide which of the given Conclusions logically follows/follow from the Statements, disregarding the commonly known facts:

Statement-1: All pens are books
Statement-2: No chair is a pen.
Conclusion-I: All chairs are books.
Conclusion-II: Some chairs are pens.
Conclusion-III: All books are chairs.
Conclusion-IV: No chair is a book.
Which one of the following is correct?

(a) Only Conclusion-I
(b) Only Conclusion-II
(c) Both Conclusion-III and Conclusion-IV
(d) None of the Conclusions follows

39. Three Statements followed by three Conclusions are given below. You have to take the Statements to be true even if they seem to be at variance from the commonly known facts. Read all the Conclusions and then decide which of the given Conclusions logically follows/follow from the Statements, disregarding the commonly known facts:

Statement-1: Some doctors are teachers.
Statement-2: All teachers are engineers.
Statement-3: All engineers are scientists.
Conclusion-I: Some scientists are doctors.
Conclusion-II: All engineers are doctors.
Conclusion-III: Some engineers are doctors.

Which one of the following is correct?
(a) Only Conclusion-I
(b) Only Conclusion-II
(c) Both Conclusion-I and Conclusion-III
(d) Both Conclusion-I and Conclusion-II

40. **Eight students A, B, C, D, E, F, G and H sit around a circular table, equidistant from each other, facing the centre of the table, not necessarily in the same order. B and D sit neither adjacent to C nor opposite to C. A sits in between E and D, and F sits in between B and H. Which one of the following is definitely correct?**
(a) B sits in between A and G
(b) C sits opposite to G
(c) E sits opposite to F
(d) None of the above

Directions for the following 4 (four) items:

Read the following two passages and answer the items that follow the passages. Your answers to these items should be based on the passages only.

Passage—1

For two or three generations past, ever-increasing numbers of individuals have been living as workers merely, not as human beings. An excessive amount of labour is rule today in every circle of society, with the result that man's spiritual element cannot thrive. He finds it very difficult to spend his little leisure in serious activities. He does not want to think; or he cannot even if he wants to. He seeks not self-improvement, but entertainment which would enable him to be mentally idle and to forget his usual activities. Therefore, the so-called culture of our age is dependant more on cinema than on theatre, more on newspapers, magazines and crime stories than on serious literature.

41. **The passage is based on the idea that**
(a) man should not work hard
(b) the great evil of our age is overstrain
(c) man cannot think well
(d) man cannot care for his spiritual welfare

42. Man does not seek self-improvement because he

(a) is not intellectually capable
(b) has no time to do so
(c) is distracted by materialism
(d) loves amusement and is mentally idle

Passage – 2

The demographic dividend, which has begun in India and is expected to last another few decades, is a great window of opportunity. The demographic dividend is basically a swelling in the working age population, which conversely means that the relative ratio of very young and very old will, for a while, be on the decline. From the experience of Ireland and China, we know that this can be a source of energy and an engine of economic growth. The demographic dividend tends to raise a nation's savings rate since in any nation, it is the working age population that is the main saver. And since the savings rate is an important driver of growth, this should help elevate our growth rate. However, the benefits of demographic dividend depend on the quality of the working age population. And this implies bringing back the importance of education, acquisition of skills and human capital.

43. Which of the following would invariably happen in a country, when the demographic dividend has begun to operate?

1. The number of illiterate people will decrease.

2. The ratio of very old and very young will decrease for a while.

3. Population growth rate will quickly stabilise.

Select the correct answer using the code given below.

(a) 1 and 2 only (b) 2 only
(c) 1 and 3 only (d) 1, 2 and 3

44. With reference to the passage, which of the following inferences can be drawn?

1. Demographic dividend is an essential condition for a country to rapidly increase its economic growth rate.

2. **Promotion of higher education is an essential condition for a country for its rapid economic growth.**

Select the correct answer using the code given below.

(a) 1 only (b) 2 only

(c) Both 1 and 2 (d) Neither 1 nor 2

45. Five friends P, Q, X, Y and Z purchased some notebooks. The relevant information is given below:

1. **Z purchased 8 notebooks more than X did.**
2. **P and Q together purchased 21 notebooks.**
3. **Q purchased 5 notebooks less than P did.**
4. **X and Y together purchased 28 notebooks.**
5. **P purchased 5 notebooks more than X did.**

If each notebook is priced ₹40, then what is the total cost of all the notebooks?

(a) ₹2,600 (b) ₹2,400

(c) ₹2,360 (d) ₹2,320

46. A man started from home at 14:30 hours and drove to village, arriving there when the village clock indicated 15:15 hours. After staying for 25 minutes, he drove back by a different route of length 1.25 times the first route at a rate twice as fast reaching home at 16:00 hours. As compared to the clock at home, the village clock is

(a) 10 minutes slow (b) 5 minutes slow

(c) 10 minutes fast (d) 5 minutes fast

47. A person X wants to distribute some pens among six children A, B, C, D, E and F. Suppose A gets twice the number of pens received by B, three times that of C, four times that of D, five times that of E and six times that of F. What is the minimum number of pens X should buy so that the number of pens each one gets is an even number?

(a) 147 (b) 150

(c) 294 (d) 300

48. Six persons A, B, C, D, E and F are sitting equidistant from each other around a circular table (facing the centre of the table).

Consider the Question and two Statements given below:

Question: Who is sitting on the immediate left of A?
Statement-1: B is sitting opposite to C and D is sitting opposite to E.
Statement-2: F is sitting on the immediate left of B.
Which one of the following is correct in respect of the Question and the Statements?

(a) Statement-1 alone is sufficient to answer the Question
(b) Statement-2 alone is sufficient to answer the Question
(c) Both Statement-1 and Statement-2 are sufficient to answer the Question
(d) Both Statement-1 and Statement-2 are not sufficient to answer the Question

49. Consider the Question and two Statements given below:
Question: What is the age of Manisha?
Statement-1: Manisha is 24 years younger than her mother.
Statement-2: 5 years later, the ages of Manisha and her mother will be in the ratio 3:5.
Which one of the following is correct in respect of the Question and the Statements?

(a) Statement-1 alone is sufficient to answer the Question
(b) Statement-2 alone is sufficient to answer the Question
(c) Both Statement-1 and Statement-2 are sufficient to answer the Question
(d) Both Statement-1 and Statement-2 are not sufficient to answer the Question

50. Six lectures A, B, C, D, E and F, each of one hour duration, are scheduled between 8:00 a.m. and 2:00 p.m. Consider the Question and two Statements given below:
Question: Which lecture is in the third period?
Statement-1: Lecture F is preceded by A and followed by C.
Statement-2: There is no lecture after lecture B.
Which one of the following is correct in respect of the Question and the Statements?

(a) Statement-1 alone is sufficient to answer the Question
(b) Statement-2 alone is sufficient to answer the Question

(c) Both Statement-1 and Statement-2 are sufficient to answer the Question
(d) Both Statement-1 and Statement-2 are not sufficient to answer the Question

Directions for the following 3 (three) items:
Read the following two passages and answer the items that follow the passages. Your answers to these items should be based on the passages only.

Passage – 1

In an economic organisation, allowing mankind to benefit by the productivity of machines should lead to a very good life of leisure, and much leisure is apt to be tedious except to those who have intelligent activities and interests. If a leisured population is to be happy, it must be an educated population, and must be educated with a view to enjoyment as well as to the direct usefulness of technical knowledge.

51. Which of the following statements best reflects the underlying tone of the passage?
(a) Only an educated population can best make use of the benefits of economic progress.
(b) All economic development should be aimed at the creation of leisure.
(c) An increase in the educated population of a country leads to an increase in the happiness of its people.
(d) Use of machines should be encouraged in order to create a large leisured population.

Passage – 2

If presents bring less thrill now that we are grown up, perhaps it is because we have too much already; or perhaps it is because we have lost the fullness of the joy of giving, and with it the fullness of the joy of receiving. Children's fears are poignant, their miseries are acute, but they do not look too forward nor too far backward. Their joys are clear and complete, because they have not yet learnt always to add 'but' to every proposition. Perhaps we are too cautious, too anxious, too sceptical. Perhaps some of our cares would shrink if we thought less about them and entered with more single-minded enjoyment into the happiness that come our way.

52. With reference to the passage, which one of the following statements is correct?

(a) It is not possible for adults to feel thrilled by presents.
(b) There can be more than one reason why adults feel less thrilled by presents.
(c) The author does not know why adults feel less thrilled by presents.
(d) Adults have less capacity to feel the joy of loving or being loved.

53. The author of the passage is against

(a) worrying too much about the past and future
(b) being in the habit of thinking about presents
(c) not being thrilled by new things
(d) giving and receiving joy only partially

54. Let A, B and C represent distinct non-zero digits. Suppose x is the sum of all possible 3-digit numbers formed by A, B and C without repetition.

Consider the following statements:

1. The 4-digit least value of x is 1332.

2. The 3-digit greatest value of x is 888.

Which of the above statements is/are correct?

(a) 1 only
(b) 2 only
(c) Both 1 and 2
(d) Neither 1 nor 2

55. There is a numeric lock which has a 3-digit PIN. The PIN contains digits 1 to 7. There is no repetition of digits. The digits in the PIN from left to right are in decreasing order. Any two digits in the PIN differ by at least 2. How many maximum attempts does one need to find out the PIN with certainty?

(a) 6
(b) 8
(c) 10
(d) 12

56. There are eight equidistant points on a circle. How many right-angled triangles can be drawn using these points as vertices and taking the diameter as one side of the triangle?

(a) 24 (b) 16
(c) 12 (d) 8

57. 24 men and 12 women can do a piece of work in 30 days. In how many days can 12 men and 24 women do the same piece of work?

(a) 30 days
(b) More than 30 days
(c) Less than 30 days or more than 30 days
(d) Data is inadequate to draw any conclusion

58. What is the remainder when 91 × 92 × 93 × 94 × 95 × 96 × 97 × 98 × 99 is divided by 1261?

(a) 3 (b) 2
(c) 1 (d) 0

59. Consider the following statements in respect of a rectangular sheet of length 20 cm and breadth 8 cm:

1. It is possible to cut the sheet exactly into 4 square sheets.

2. It is possible to cut the sheet into 10 triangular sheets of equal area.

Which of the above statements is/are correct?

(a) 1 only (b) 2 only
(c) Both 1 and 2 (d) Neither 1 nor 2

60. When 70% of a number x is added to another number y, the sum becomes 165% of the value of y. When 60% of the number x is added to another number z, then the sum becomes 165% of the value of z. Which one of the following is correct?

(a) $z<x<y$ (b) $x<y<z$
(c) $y<x<z$ (d) $z<y<x$

Directions for the following 3 (three) items:

Read the following two passages and answer the items that follow the passages. Your answers to these items should be based on the passages only.

Passage—1

The majority of people who fail to accumulate money sufficient for their needs, are generally, easily influenced by the opinions of others. They permit the newspapers and the gossiping neighbours to do their thinking for them. Opinions are the cheapest commodities on the earth. Everyone has a flock of opinions ready to be wished upon by anyone who will accept them. If you are influenced by opinions when you reach decisions, you will not succeed in any undertaking.

61. Which one of the following is implied by the passage?

(a) Most of the people do not accumulate money for their needs.

(b) Most of the people never fail to accumulate money for their needs.

(c) There are people who fail to accumulate money for their needs.

(d) There is no need to accumulate money.

62. What is the main idea of the passage?

(a) People should not be influenced by the opinions of others.

(b) People should accumulate as much money as they can.

(c) People should neither give nor accept the opinions.

(d) People will succeed in any undertaking if they do not accept any opinion at all.

Passage – 2

"The social order is a sacred right which is the basis of all other rights. Nevertheless, this right does not come from nature, and must therefore be founded on conventions."

63. With reference to the above passage, which of the following statements is/are correct?

1. Conventions are the sources of rights of man.

2. Rights of man can be exercised only when there is a social order.

Select the correct answer using the code given below.

(a) 1 only

(b) 2 only

(c) Both 1 and 2

(d) Neither I nor 2

64. Two candidates X and Y contested an election. 80% of voters cast their vote and there were no invalid votes. There was no NOTA (None of the above) option. X got 56% of the votes cast and won by 1440 votes. What is the total number of voters in the voters list?

(a) 15000 (b) 12000
(c) 9600 (d) 5000

65. What is the smallest number greater than 1000 that when divided by any one of the numbers 6, 9, 12, 15, 18 leaves a remainder of 3?

(a) 1063 (b) 1073
(c) 1083 (d) 1183

66. Let p be a two-digit number and q be the number consisting of same digits written in reverse order. If p×q = 2430, then what is the difference between p and q?

(a) 45 (b) 27
(c) 18 (d) 9

67. Consider the following statements in respect of two natural numbers p and q such that p is a prime number and q is a composite number:

1. p×q can be an odd number.
2. q/p can be a prime number.
3. p+q can be a prime number.

Which of the above statements are correct?

(a) 1 and 2 only (b) 2 and 3 only
(c) 1 and 3 only (d) 1, 2 and 3

68. Consider the following statements:

1. Between 3:16 p.m. and 3:17 p.m., both hour hand and minute hand coincide.
2. Between 4:58 p.m. and 4:59 p.m., both minute hand and second hand coincide.

Which of the above statements is/are correct?

(a) 1 only
(b) 2 only
(c) Both 1 and 2
(d) Neither 1 nor 2

69. There are two containers X and Y. X contains 100 ml of milk and Y contains 100 ml of water. 20 ml of milk from X is transferred to Y. After mixing well, 20 ml of the mixture in Y is transferred back to X. If m denotes the proportion of milk in X and n denotes the proportion of water in Y, then which one of the following is correct?

(a) $m = n$
(b) $m > n$
(c) $m < n$
(d) Cannot be determined due to insufficient data

70. A pie chart gives the expenditure on five different items A, B, C, D and E in a household. If B, C, D and E correspond to 90°, 50°, 45° and 75° respectively, then what is the percentage of expenditure on item A?

(a) $\frac{112}{9}$ (b) $\frac{125}{6}$

(c) $\frac{155}{9}$ (d) $\frac{250}{9}$

Directions for the following 3 (three) items:

Read the following two passages and answer the items that follow the passages. Your answers to these items should be based on the passages only.

Passage – 1

To encourage research is one of the functions of a university. Contemporary universities have encouraged research, not only in those cases where research is necessary, but on all sorts of entirely unprofitable subjects as well. Scientific research is probably never completely valueless. However silly and insignificant it may seem, however mechanical and unintelligent the labours of the researchers, there is always a chance that the results may be of value to the investigator of talent, who can use the facts collected for him by uninspired but industrious researchers as the basis of some fruitful generalisation. But where research is not original, but consists in the mere rearrangement of existing materials, where its object is not scientific but literary or historical, then there is a risk of the whole business becoming merely futile.

71. The author's assumption about scientific research is that

(a) it is never very valuable
(b) it is sometimes very valuable
(c) it is never without some value
(d) it is always very valuable

72. According to the author

(a) not many research results can be of value to an intelligent investigator
(b) a research result is always valuable to an intelligent investigator
(c) any research result can be of value to an intelligent investigator
(d) a research result must always be of some value to an intelligent investigator

Passage – 2

How best can the problems of floods and droughts be addressed so that the losses are minimal and the system becomes resilient? In this context, one important point that needs to be noted is that India gets 'too much' water (about 75% of annual precipitation) during 120 days (June to September) and 'too little' for the remaining 245 days. This skewed water availability has to be managed and regulated for its consumption throughout the year.

73. Which one of the following best reflects the practical, rational and lasting solution?

(a) Constructing huge concrete storage tanks and canals across the country
(b) Changing the cropping patterns and farming practices
(c) Interlinking of rivers across the country
(d) Buffer stocking of water through dams and recharging aquifers

74. If 15 × 14 × 13 ×...× 3 × 2 × 1 = 3^m × n where m and n are positive integers, then what is the maximum value of m?

(a) 7 (b) 6
(c) 5 (d) 4

75. What is the value of X in the sequence 2, 12, 36, 80, 150, X?

(a) 248 (b) 252
(c) 258 (d) 262

76. One non-zero digit, one vowel and one consonant from English alphabet (in capital) are to be used in forming passwords, such that each password has to start with a vowel and end with a consonant. How many such passwords can be generated?

(a) 105 (b) 525
(c) 945 (d) 1050

77. There are 9 cups placed on a table arranged in equal number of rows and columns out of which 6 cups contain coffee and 3 cups contain tea. In how many ways can they be arranged so that each row should contain at least one cup of coffee?

(a) 18 (b) 27
(c) 54 (d) 81

78. The sum of three consecutive integers is equal to their product. How many such possibilities are there?

(a) Only one (b) Only two
(c) Only three (d) No such possibility is there

79. What is the number of numbers of the form 0. XY, where X and Y are distinct non-zero digits?

(a) 72 (b) 81
(c) 90 (d) 100

80. The average weight of A, B, C is 40 kg, the average weight of B, D, E is 42 kg and the weight of F is equal to that of B. What is the average weight of A, B, C, D, E and F?

(a) 40.5 kg
(b) 40.8 kg
(c) 41 kg
(d) Cannot be determined as data is inadequate

Answers

1. (a)	**2.** (a)	**3.** (c)	**4.** (d)	**5.** (a)	**6.** (a)	**7.** (d)	**8.** (d)
9. (b)	**10.** (c)	**11.** (b)	**12.** (d)	**13.** (a)	**14.** (a)	**15.** (b)	**16.** (d)
17. (c)	**18.** (b)	**19.** (d)	**20.** (b)	**21.** (d)	**22.** (a)	**23.** (d)	**24.** (c)
25. (d)	**26.** (b)	**27.** (c)	**28.** (d)	**29.** (c)	**30.** (a)	**31.** (c)	**32.** (c)
33. (a)	**34.** (d)	**35.** (d)	**36.** (d)	**37.** (d)	**38.** (d)	**39.** (c)	**40.** (d)
41. (b)	**42.** (b)	**43.** (b)	**44.** (d)	**45.** (a)	**46.** (d)	**47.** (c)	**48.** (d)
49. (c)	**50.** (d)	**51.** (a)	**52.** (b)	**53.** (a)	**54.** (a)	**55.** (c)	**56.** (a)
57. (d)	**58.** (c)	**59.** (c)	**60.** (a)	**61.** (c)	**62.** (a)	**63.** (c)	**64.** (a)
65. (c)	**66.** (c)	**67.** (d)	**68.** (c)	**69.** (a)	**70.** (d)	**71.** (c)	**72.** (c)
73. (d)	**74.** (b)	**75.** (b)	**76.** (c)	**77.** (d)	**78.** (c)	**79.** (a)	**80.** (c)

मुख्य परीक्षा-2022

हिंदी (अनिवार्य)

1. निम्नलिखित में से किसी एक विषय पर लगभग 600 शब्दों में निबंध लिखिए-

(a) नवीकरणीय ऊर्जा : संभावनाएँ और चुनौतियाँ

(b) संचार क्रांति का महत्त्व

(c) खेलों का बढ़ता व्यवसायीकरण

(d) खान-पान का स्वास्थ्य पर प्रभाव

2. निम्नलिखित गद्यांश को ध्यानपूर्वक पढ़िए और उसके आधार पर नीचे दिए गए प्रश्नों के उत्तर स्पष्ट, सही और संक्षिप्त भाषा में दीजिए-

औपनिवेशिक शासन बेहिसाब आँकड़ों और जानकारियों के संग्रह पर आधारित था। अंग्रेजों ने अपने व्यावसायिक मामलों को चलाने के लिए व्यापारिक गतिविधियों का विस्तृत ब्यौरा रखा था। बढ़ते शहरों में जीवन की गति और दिशा पर नजर रखने के लिए वे नियमित रूप से सर्वेक्षण करते थे, सांख्यिकीय आँकड़े इकट्ठा करते थे और विभिन्न प्रकार की सरकारी रिपोर्टें प्रकाशित करते थे।

प्रारंभिक वर्षों से ही औपनिवेशिक सरकार ने मानचित्र तैयार करने पर खास ध्यान

दिया। सरकार का मानना था कि किसी जगह की बनावट और भूदृश्य को समझने के लिए नक्शे जरूरी होते हैं। इस जानकारी के सहारे वे इलाके पर ज्यादा बेहतर नियंत्रण कायम कर सकते थे। जब शहर बढ़ने लगे तो न केवल उनके विकास की योजना तैयार करने के लिए, बल्कि व्यवसाय को विकसित करने और अपनी सत्ता मजबूत करने के लिए भी नक्शे बनाए जाने लगे। शहरों के नक्शों से हमें उस स्थान पर पहाड़ियों, नदियों व हरियाली का पता चलता है। ये सारी चीजें रक्षा संबंधी उद्देश्यों के लिए योजना तैयार करने में बहुत काम आती हैं। इसके अलावा घाटों की जगह, मकानों की सघनता और गुणवत्ता तथा सड़कों की स्थिति आदि से इलाके की व्यावसायिक संभावनाओं का पता लगाने और कराधान (टैक्स व्यवस्था) की रणनीति बनाने में मदद मिलती है।

उन्नीसवीं सदी के आखिर से अंग्रेजों ने वार्षिक नगरपालिका कर वसूली के जरिए शहरों के रखरखाव के वास्ते पैसा इकट्ठा करने की कोशिशें शुरू कर दी थीं। टकरावों से बचने के लिए उन्होंने कुछ जिम्मेदारियाँ निर्वाचित भारतीय प्रतिनिधियों को भी सौंपी हुई थीं। आंशिक लोक प्रतिनिधित्व से लैस नगर निगम जैसे संस्थानों का उद्देश्य शहरों में जलापूर्ति, निकासी, सड़क निर्माण और स्वास्थ्य व्यवस्था जैसी अत्यावश्यक सेवाएँ उपलब्ध कराना था। दूसरी तरफ, नगर निगमों की गतिविधियों से नए तरह के रिकॉड्र्स पैदा हुए जिन्हें नगरपालिका रिकॉर्ड रूम में सँभालकर रखा जाने लगा।

शहरों के फैलाव पर नजर रखने के लिए नियमित रूप से लोगों की गिनती की जाती थी। उन्नीसवीं सदी के मध्य तक विभिन्न क्षेत्रों में कई जगह स्थानीय स्तर पर जनगणना की जा चुकी थी। अखिल भारतीय जनगणना का पहला प्रयास 1872 में किया गया। इसके बाद, 1881 से दशकीय (हर 10 साल में होने वाली) जनगणना एक नियमित व्यवस्था बन गई। भारत में शहरीकरण का अध्ययन करने के लिए जनगणना से निकले आँकड़े एक बहुमूल्य स्रोत हैं।

जब हम इन रिपोर्टों को देखते हैं तो ऐसा लगता है कि हमारे पास ऐतिहासिक परिवर्तन को मापने के लिए ठोस जानकारी उपलब्ध हैं। बीमारियों से होने वाली मौतों की सारणियों का अंतहीन सिलसिला या उम्र, लिंग, जाति एवं व्यवसाय के अनुसार लोगों को गिनने की व्यवस्था से संख्याओं का एक विशाल भंडार मिलता है जिससे सटीकता का भ्रम पैदा हो जाता है। लेकिन इतिहासकारों ने पाया है कि ये आँकड़े भ्रामक भी हो सकते हैं। इन आँकड़ों का इस्तेमाल करने से पहले हमें इस बात को अच्छी तरह समझ लेना चाहिए कि आँकड़े किसने इकट्ठा किए हैं और उन्हें क्यों तथा कैसे इकट्ठा किया गया था। हमें यह भी मालूम होना चाहिए कि किस चीज को मापा गया था और किस चीज को नहीं मापा गया था।

(a) औपनिवेशिक शासन चलाने में आँकड़ों का क्या महत्त्व था?

(b) औपनिवेशिक शासकों के लिए मानचित्र क्यों महत्त्वपूर्ण थे?

(c) औपनिवेशिक अभिलेखों के माध्यम से शहरीकरण का अध्ययन किस प्रकार किया जा सकता है?

(d) इतिहासकार आँकड़ों को सदैव अहानिकर क्यों नहीं मानते?

(e) औपनिवेशिक शासकों की करों से संबंधित नीति क्या थी?

3. निम्नलिखित अनुच्छेद का संक्षेपण लगभग एक-तिहाई शब्दों में लिखिए। इसका शीर्षक लिखने की आवश्यकता नहीं है। संक्षेपण अपने शब्दों में ही लिखिए-

साधारणतया 'विकास' शब्द से अभिप्राय समाज विशेष की स्थिति और उसके द्वारा अनुभव किए गए परिवर्तन की प्रक्रिया से होता है। मानव इतिहास के लंबे अंतराल में समाज और उसके जैव-भौतिक पर्यावरण की निरंतर अंत: क्रियाएँ समाज की स्थिति का निर्धारण करती हैं। मानव और पर्यावरण अंत: क्रिया की प्रक्रियाएँ इस बात पर निर्भर करती हैं कि समाज ने किस प्रकार की प्रौद्योगिकी विकसित की है और किस प्रकार की संस्थाओं का पोषण किया है। प्रौद्योगिकी और संस्थाओं ने मानव-पर्यावरण अंत:क्रिया को गति प्रदान की है तो इससे पैदा हुए संवेग ने प्रौद्योगिकी का स्तर ऊँचा उठाया है और अनेक संस्थाओं का निर्माण और रूपांतरण किया है। अत: विकास एक बहु-आयामी संकल्पना है और अर्थव्यवस्था, समाज तथा पर्यावरण में सकारात्मक व अनुत्क्रमणीय परिवर्तन का द्योतक है।

विकास की संकल्पना गतिक है और इस संकल्पना का प्रादुर्भाव 20वीं शताब्दी के उत्तरार्ध में हुआ है। द्वितीय विश्व युद्ध के उपरांत विकास की संकल्पना आर्थिक वृद्धि की पर्याय थी जिसे सकल राष्ट्रीय उत्पाद, प्रति व्यक्ति आय और प्रति व्यक्ति उपभोग में समय के साथ बढ़ोतरी के रूप में मापा जाता है। परंतु अधिक आर्थिक वृद्धि वाले देशों में भी असमान वितरण के कारण गरीबी का स्तर बहुत तेजी से बढ़ा। अत: 1970 के दशक में 'पुनर्वितरण के साथ वृद्धि' तथा 'वृद्धि और समानता' जैसे वाक्यांश विकास की परिभाषा में शामिल किए गए। पुनर्वितरण और समानता के प्रश्नों से निपटते हुए यह अनुभव हुआ कि विकास की संकल्पना को मात्र आर्थिक प्रक्षेत्र तक ही सीमित नहीं रखा जा सकता। इसमें लोगों के कल्याण और रहने के स्तर, जन स्वास्थ्य, शिक्षा, समान अवसर और राजनीतिक तथा नागरिक अधिकारों से संबंधित मुद्दे भी सम्मिलित हैं। 1980 के दशक तक विकास एक बहु-आयामी संकल्पना के रूप में उभरा जिसमें समाज के सभी लोगों के लिए वृहद स्तर पर सामाजिक एवं भौतिक कल्याण का समावेश है।

1960 के दशक के अंत में पश्चिमी दुनिया में पर्यावरण संबंधी मुद्दों पर बढ़ती जागरूकता की सामान्य वृद्धि के कारण सतत पोषणीय धारणा का विकास हुआ। इससे पर्यावरण पर औद्योगिक विकास के अनापेक्षित प्रभावों के विषय में लोगों की चिंता प्रकट होती थी।

पर्यावरणीय मुद्दों पर विश्व समुदाय की बढ़ती चिंता को ध्यान में रखकर संयुक्त राष्ट्र संघ ने 'विश्व पर्यावरण और विकास आयोग (WCED)' की स्थापना की जिसकी प्रमुख नार्वे की प्रधानमंत्री ग्रो हरलेम ब्रेटलैंड थीं। इस आयोग ने अपनी रिपोर्ट 'अवर कॉमन फ्यूचर' (जिसे ब्रंटलैंड रिपोर्ट भी कहते हैं) 1987 में प्रस्तुत की। WCED ने सतत पोषणीय विकास की सीधी-सरल और वृहद स्तर पर प्रयुक्त परिभाषा प्रस्तुत की। इस रिपोर्ट के अनुसार सतत पोषणीय विकास का अर्थ है- "एक ऐसा विकास जिसमें भविष्य में आने वाली पीढ़ियों की आवश्यकता पूर्ति को प्रभावित किए बिना वर्तमान पीढ़ी द्वारा अपनी आवश्यकता की पूर्ति करना।"

4. निम्नलिखित गद्यांश का अंग्रेजी में अनुवाद कीजिए-

प्रेमचंद ने कहा था कि कहानियाँ तो चारों तरफ हवा में बिखरी पड़ी हैं, सवाल उन्हें पकड़ने का है। ऐसा इसलिए है कि हर व्यक्ति और हर वस्तु का अपना-अपना जीवन होता है, बाकी सबसे अलग। उसका एक आरंभ, विकास और फिर अंत भी होता है। सबकी कोई-न-कोई कहानी होती है। जिस तरह एक व्यक्ति दूसरे से हू-ब-हू नहीं मिलता, वैसे ही उसकी अपनी जीवन-कथा भी दूसरे से नहीं मिलती। ऐसा कोई व्यक्ति नहीं है जो अपनी कथा न लिख सके। मेरी आत्मकथा मेरे जीवन की कथा है। यह केवल मेरी कथा है। और जहाँ तक मेरा जीवन दूसरों के जीवन को छूता है, वहाँ तक यह दूसरों की भी कथा है। और जहाँ तक मेरा जीवन एक समय, समाज या समूह का प्रतिनिधि जीवन होता है, वहाँ तक वह सबकी कथा बन जाती है। प्रत्येक व्यक्ति का जीवन कथा में बदलने के योग्य है।

आप कलम हाथ में लेते हैं और कागज पर कुछ लिखने लगते हैं। सबसे अच्छा है अपने ही जीवन से शुरू किया जाए। अपने बारे में, बचपन से लेकर अब तक जो-जो हुआ, वह सब। यही तो आत्मकथा है। आत्मकथा की पहली शर्त है साफ-साफ, सच-सच कहना।

इसके लिए भी अभ्यास जरूरी है। नैतिक साहस जरूरी है। अगर पूरी आत्मकथा न भी लिखी जाए तो संस्मरण या डायरी लिखी जा सकती है। कई दिनों वर्षों की डायरी आत्मकथा बन जाती है।

5. **निम्नलिखित गद्यांश का हिंदी में अनुवाद कीजिए-**

Socrates was one of the celebrated Greek thinkers who became very influential in the development of Greek philosophy in particular and Western philosophy in general.

Socrates tried to bring radical changes in the society. But his attempts in the social field were not accepted and appreciated by the authorities. But convinced of his principles Socrates continued his efforts. The authorities considered him as a threat to their existence and as a result he was arrested and sent to prison. Later, he was given capital punishment because he was frank and outspoken. When he received the news of the death penalty he was not at all shaken.

It confused all the officials and even Socrates' own disciples because they had never seen a person accepting the news of his death penalty with a smiling face. When asked why so, he replied, "I have been preparing for death all my life. I have never done anything wrong to any man. That is why I am able to accept even death with a smiling face."

In his use of critical reasoning, by his unwavering commitment to truth and through the vivid example of his own life, Socrates set the standard for all subsequent Western philosophy.

6. (a) **निम्नलिखित मुहावरों का अर्थ स्पष्ट करते हुए उनका वाक्यों में प्रयोग कीजिए-**

(i) नाक पर मक्खी न बैठने देना

(ii) छाती पर साँप लोटना

(iii) बंदर घुड़की देना

(iv) गिन-गिनकर पैर रखना

(v) मिट्टी में मिलना

(b) **निम्नलिखित वाक्यों के शुद्ध रूप लिखिए-**

(i) कई रेलवे के कर्मचारियों ने अवकाश लिया।

(ii) साहित्य और समाज का घोर संबंध है।

(iii) तब शायद यह काम जरूर हो जाएगा।

(iv) लड़का मिठाई लेकर भागता हुआ घर आया।
(v) हमारे यहाँ तरुण नवयुवकों की शिक्षा का अच्छा प्रबंध है।

(c) निम्नलिखित शब्दों के दो-दो पर्यायवाची लिखिए-

(i) स्वर्ण
(ii) सूर्य
(iii) हिमालय
(iv) हाथी
(v) अमृत

(d) निम्नलिखित युग्मों को इस तरह से वाक्य में प्रयुक्त कीजिए कि उनका अर्थ एवं अंतर स्पष्ट हो जाए-

(i) आदि-आदी
(ii) क्रांति—क्लांति
(iii) नियत — नियति
(iv) प्रणय-परिणय
(v) वित्त वृत्त

Main Exam—2022

English (Compulsory)

1. Write an essay in about 600 words on any one of the following topics:

(a) Mathematics: A mirror of modern civilisation.
(b) New frontiers of science need to be explored in the current times.
(c) Education is a means of shaping character and of social change.
(d) The role of literature in a common man's life.

2. Read carefully the passage given below and write your answers to the questions that follow in clear, correct and concise language:

Not so long ago a book on human origins would have devoted a substantial number of pages to descriptions of the fossil evidence for primate evolution. This was in part because it was assumed that at each stage of primate evolution one of the fossil primates would have been recognizable as the direct ancestor of modern humans. However, we now know that for various reasons many of these tax a are highly unlikely to be ancestral to living higher primates. Instead, this account will concentrate on what we know of the evolution and relationships of the great apes. It will review how long Western scientists have known about the great apes, and it will show how ideas about their relationships to each other, and to modern humans, have changed. It will also explore which of the living apes is most closely related to modern humans.

Among the tales of exotic animals brought home by explorers and traders were descriptions of what we now know as the great apes, that is, chimpanzees and gorillas from Africa, and orangutans from Asia. Aristotle referred to 'apes' as well as to 'monkeys' and 'baboons' in his *Historia animalium* (literally the 'History of Animals'), but his 'apes' were the same as the 'apes' dissected by the early anatomists, which were short-tailed macaque monkeys from North Africa. One of the first people to undertake a systematic review of the differences between modern humans and the chimpanzee and gorilla was Thomas Henry Huxley. In an essay entitled 'On the relations of Man to the Lower Animals' that formed the central section of his 1863 book called *Evidence as to Man's Place in Nature*, he concluded the anatomical differences between modern humans and the chimpanzee and gorilla were less marked than the differences between the two African apes and the orangutan.

Darwin used this evidence in his *The Descent of Man* published in 1871 to suggest that, because the African apes were morphologically closer to modern humans than to the only great ape known from Asia, the ancestors of modern humans were more likely to be found in Africa than elsewhere. This deduction played a critical role in pointing most researchers towards Africa as a likely place to find human ancestors. As we will see in the next chapter, those who considered the orangutan our closest relative looked to South-East Asia as the most likely place to find modern human ancestors.

Developments in biochemistry and immunology during the first half of the 20th century allowed the search for evidence about the nature of the relationships between modern humans and the apes to be shifted from traditional morphology to the morphology of molecules. The earliest attempts to use proteins to determine primate relationships were made just after the turn of the century, but the first results of a new generation of analyses were reported in the early 1960s. The famous US biochemist Linus Pauling coined the name 'molecular anthropology' for this area of research. Two reports, both published in 1963, provided crucial evidence. Emile Zuckerkandl, another pioneer molecular anthropologist, described how he used enzymes to break up the protein haemoglobin from blood red cells into its peptide components, and that when he separated them using a small electric current, the patterns made by the peptides from a modern human, a chimpanzee, and a gorilla were indistinguishable. The second contribution was by Morris Goodman, who has spent his life working on molecular anthropology, who used techniques borrowed from immunology to study samples of a serum (serum is what is left after blood has clotted) protein called albumin taken from modern humans, apes and monkeys. He came to the conclusion that the albumins of modern humans and chimpanzees were so alike in their structure that you cannot tell them apart.

Proteins are made up of a string of amino acids. In many instances one amino acid may be substituted for another without changing the function of the protein. In the 1960s and 1970s Vince Sarich and Allan Wilson, two Berkeley biochemists interested in primate and human evolution, exploited these minor variations in protein structure in order to determine the evolutionary history of the molecules, and therefore, presumably, the evolutionary history of the taxa being sampled. They, too, concluded that modern humans and the African apes were very closely related.

(a) What does the author say about earlier assumptions regarding evolution?

(b) According to the author, how are modern humans and apes related?

(c) What later developments took place in the twentieth century in investigating the relationship of apes and humans?
(d) What were the attempts made to use proteins to determine primate relationships?
(e) In what way does the latest research prove the relationship between apes and humans?

3. Make a précis of the following passage in about one-third of its length. Do not give a title to it. The précis should be written in your own language:

Everyone must have had at least one personal experience with a computer error by this time. Bank balances are suddenly reported to have jumped into the millions, appeals for charitable contributions are mailed over and over to people with crazy-sounding names at your address, department stores send the wrong bills, utility companies write that they're turning everything off, that sort of thing. If you manage to get in touch with someone and complain, you then get instantaneously typed, guilty letters from the same computer, saying, 'Our computer was in error, and an adjustment is being made in your account.'

These are supposed to be the sheerest and blindest accidents. Mistakes are not believed to be part of the normal behavior of a good machine. If things go wrong, it must be a personal, human error, the result of fingering, tampering, a button getting stuck, someone hitting the wrong key. The computer, at its normal best, is infallible.

I wonder whether this can be true. After all, the whole point of computers is that they represent an extension of the human brain, vastly improved upon but nonetheless human, super-human maybe. A good computer can think clearly and quickly enough to beat you at chess, and some of them have even been programmed to write obscure verse. They can do anything we can do, and more besides.

It is not yet known whether a computer has its own consciousness, and it would be hard to find out about this. When you walk into one of those great halls now built for the huge machines, and stand listening, it is easy to imagine that the faint, distant noises are the sound of thinking, and the turning of the spools gives them the look of wild creatures rolling their eyes in the effort to concentrate, choking with information. But real thinking, and dreaming, are other matters.

On the other hand, the evidences of something like an unconscious, equivalent to ours, are all around, in every mail. As extensions of the human brain, they have been constructed with the same property of error, spontaneous, uncontrolled, and rich in possibilities.

Mistakes are at the very base of human thought, embedded there, feeding the structure like root nodules. If we were not provided with the knack of being wrong, we could never get anything useful done. We think our way along by choosing between right and wrong alternatives, and the wrong choices have to be made as frequently as the right ones. We get along in life this way. We are built to make mistakes, coded for error.

We learn, as we say, by 'trial and error'. Why do we always say that? Why not 'trial and rightness' or 'trial and triumph' ? The old phrase puts it that way because that is, in real life, the way it is done.

A good laboratory, like a good bank or a corporation or government, has to run like a computer. Almost everything is done flawlessly, by the book, and all the numbers add up to the predicted sums. The days go by. And then, if it is a lucky day, and a lucky laboratory, somebody makes a mistake: the wrong buffer, something in one of the blanks, a decimal misplaced in reading counts, the warm room off by a degree and a half, a mouse out of his box, or just a misreading of the day's protocol. Whatever, when the results come in, something is obviously screwed up, and then the action can begin.

The misreading is not the important error; it opens the way. The next step is the crucial one. If the investigator can bring himself to say, 'But even so, look at that!' then the new finding, whatever it is, is ready for snatching. What is needed, for progress to be made, is the move based on the error.

Whenever new kinds of thinking are about to be accomplished, or new varieties of music, there has to be an argument beforehand. With two sides debating in the same mind, haranguing, there is an amiable understanding that one is right and the other wrong. Sooner or later the thing is settled, but there can be no action at all if there are not the two sides, and the argument. The hope is in the faculty of wrongness, the tendency toward error. The capacity to leap across mountains of information to land lightly on the wrong side represents the highest of human endowments.

4. (a) Rewrite the following sentences after making necessary corrections. Do not make unnecessary changes in the original sentence:

(i) Every man, woman and child were rescued.
(ii) No sooner I am out, than the students make a noise.
(iii) Walk carefully lest you may not fall.
(iv) The patient died before the doctor arrived.
(v) Time and tide waits for none.
(vi) Into what kind of mess have you got me into?
(vii) I learned the answer would come sooner than I expected.
(viii) Hardly he had stepped out than it began to rain.
(ix) Either of the five dancers will dance tonight.
(x) My client was neither aware nor party to the plot.

(b) Supply the missing words:

(i) She started the work .... a few days.
(ii) There is no exception .... this rule.
(iii) We are accountable to God .... our actions
(iv) The police is entrusted .... the enforcement of law and order.
(v) The girl was hit with a stone .... her brother.

(c) Use the correct forms of the verbs given in brackets:

(i) After she .... (take) her lunch, she went to the theatre.
(ii) The doctor ....(examine) the patients every evening.

(iii) They .... (build) that bridge since 2003.
(iv) He .... (play) cards, when I saw him.
(v) If she works hard, she .... (get) a first class.

(d) Write the antonyms of the following:

(i) Ecstasy	(ii) Advocate
(iii) Anaemic	(iv) Allow
(v) Hyperbole	

5. (a) Rewrite the following sentences as directed without changing the meaning:

(i) He is a learned man. He cannot make that mistake. (Combine the sentence by using 'too' - 'to')
(ii) Brutus was not without love for Caesar ....? (Add a question tag)
(iii) As soon as he went there, the uproar commenced. (Remove 'as soon as' and put 'no sooner than')
(iv) Either the father or the son has not taken it. (Use 'neither-nor')
(v) You tell me the truth. I shall not punish you. (Rewrite the sentence beginning with 'unless'.)
(vi) The Prince said, "It gives me great pleasure to be here this evening". (Change into Indirect Speech)
(vii) The minister was spoken to by them. (Change into active voice)
(viii) Not only Rama but also Gopal did it. (Remove 'not only' - 'but also' and put 'as well as')
(ix) The farmer worked so hard, that he might not starve. (Remove 'so' and 'that' and put 'lest')
(x) Hardly had I arrived at the gate, when my servant brought the horse. (Remove 'hardly' and put 'scarcely')

(b) Use the following words to make sentences that bring out their meaning clearly. Do not change the form of the words. (No marks will be given for vague and ambiguous sentences):

(i) Misogynist	(ii) Unprecedented
(iii) Orchard	(iv) Morale
(v) Volunteer	

(c) Choose the appropriate word to fill in the blanks:
   (i) Modern youth is fond of .... life. (ostentatious / ostensible)
   (ii) The poetry of Keats has a .... beauty. (sensational / sensuous)
   (iii) King Ashoka did not approve of the .... (barbarous / barbaric) sport of hunting behaviour. (obnoxious / noxious)
   (iv) Everyone despised him for his .... party was attacked by militants. (petrol / patrol)
   (v) The .... party was attacked by militants. (pertol/ patrol)

5. (d) Use the following idioms/phrases in sentences of your own to bring out their meaning clearly:
   (i) back seat driver
   (ii) call it a day
   (iii) wet behind the ears
   (iv) set off
   (v) run out of

UPSC CIVIL SERVICES MAINS – 2022
Essay Question Paper

Section: A

1. Forests are the best case studies for economic excellence
2. Poets are the unacknowledged legislators of the world
3. History is a series of victories won by the scientific man over the romantic man
4. A ship in harbour is safe, but that is not what ship is for

Section: B

5. The time to repair the roof is when the sun is shining
6. You cannot step twice in the same river
7. A smile is the chosen vehicle for all ambiguities
8. Just because you have a choice, it does not mean that any of them has to be right.

MAIN EXAMINATION – 2022
General Studies Paper-I

1. How will you explain the medieval Indian temple sculpture represent the social life of those days? (Answer in 150 words) 10
2. Why did armies of the British East India Company—mostly comprising of Indian soldiers—win consistently against the more numerous and better equipped armies of the Indian rulers? Give reasons. (Answer in 150 words) 10
3. Why was there a sudden spurt in famines in colonial India since the mid-eighteenth century? Give reasons. (Answer in 150 words) 10
4. Describe the characteristics and types of primary rocks. (Answer in 150 words) 10
5. Discuss the meaning of colour-coded weather warnings for cyclone prone areas given by India Meteorological department. (Answer in 150 words) 10
6. Discuss the natural resource potentials of 'Deccan trap'. (Answer in 150 words) 10
7. Examine the potential of wind energy in India and explain the reasons for their limited spatial spread. (Answer in 150 words) 10
8. Explore and evaluate the impact of 'Work From Home' on family relationships. (Answer in 150 words) 10
9. How is the growth of Tier-2 cities related to the rise of a new middle class with an emphasis on the culture of consumption? (Answer in 150 words) 10
10. Given the diversities among tribal communities in India, in which specific contexts should they be considered as a single category? (Answer in 150 words) 10
11. The political and administrative reorganisation of states and territories has been a continuous ongoing process since the mid-nineteenth century. Discuss with examples. (Answer in 250 words) 15
12. Discuss the main contributions of Gupta period and Chola period to Indian heritage and culture. (Answer in 250 words) 15

13. Discuss the significance of the lion and bull figures in Indian mythology, art and architecture. (Answer in 250 words) 15
14. What are the forces that influence ocean currents? Describe their role in fishing industry of the world. (Answer in 250 words) 15
15. Describing the distribution of rubber producing countries, indicate the major environmental issues faced by them. (Answer in 250 words) 15
16. Mention the significance of straits and isthmus in international trade. (Answer in 250 words) 15
17. Troposphere is a very significant atmospheric layer that determines weather process. How? (Answer in 250 words) 15
18. Analyse the salience of 'Sect' in Indian society vis-à-vis caste, region and religion. (Answer in 250 words) 15
19. Are tolerance, assimilation and pluralism the key elements in the making of an Indian form of secularism? Justify your answer. (Answer in 250 words) 15
20. Elucidate the relationship between globalisation and new technology in a world of scarce resources, with special reference to India. (Answer in 250 words) 15

MAIN EXAMINATION – 2022
General Studies Paper-II

1. "The most significant achievement of modern law in India is the constitutionalisation of environmental problems by the Supreme Court." Discuss this statement with the help of relevant case laws. (Answer in 150 words) 10
2. "Right of movement and residence throughout the territory of India are freely available to the Indian citizens, but these rights are not absolute." Comment. (Answer in 150 words) 10
3. To what extent, in your opinion, as the decentralisation of power in India changed the governance landscape at the grassroots? (Answer in 150 words) 10

4. Discuss the role of the Vice–President of India as the Chairman of the Rajya Sabha. (Answer in 150 words) 10

5. Discuss the role of the National Commission for Backward Classes in the wake of its transformation from a statutory body to a constitutional body. (Answer in 150 words) 10

6. The Gati-Shakti Yojana needs meticulous coordination between the government and the private sector to achieve the goal of connectivity. Discuss. (Answer in 150 words) 10

7. The Rights of Persons with Disabilities Act, 2016 remains only a legal document without intense sensitisation of government functionaries and citizens regarding disability. Comment. (Answer in 150 words) 10

8. Reforming the government delivery system through the Direct Benefit Transfer Scheme is a progressive step, but it has its limitations too. Comment. (Answer in 150 words) 10

9. 'India is an age-old friend of Sri Lanka.' Discuss India's role in the recent crisis in Sri Lanka in the light of the preceding statement. (Answer in 150 words) 10

10. Do you think that BIMSTEC is a parallel organisation like the SAARC ? What are the similarities and dissimilarities between the two? How are Indian foreign policy objectives realised by forming this new organisation? (Answer in 150 words) 10

11. Discuss the procedures to decide the disputes arising out of the election of a Member of the Parliament or State Legislature under The Representation of the People Act, 1951. What are the grounds on which the election of any returned candidate may be declared void? What remedy is available to the aggrieved party against the decision? Refer to the case laws. (Answer in 250 words) 15

12. Discuss the essential conditions for exercise of the legislative powers by the Governor. Discuss the legality of re-promulgation of ordinances by the Governor without placing them before the Legislature. (Answer in 250 words) 15

13. "While the national political parties in India favour centralisation, the regional parties are in favour of State autonomy." Comment. (Answer in 250 words) 15
14. Critically examine the procedures through which the Presidents of India and France are elected. (Answer in 250 words) 15
15. Discuss the role of the Election Commission of India in the light of the evolution of the Model Code of Conduct. (Answer in 250 words) 15
16. Besides the welfare schemes, India needs deft management of inflation and unemployment to serve the poor and the underprivileged sections of the society. Discuss. (Answer in 250 words) 15
17. Do you agree with the view that increasing dependence on donor agencies for development reduces the importance of community participation in the development process? Justify your answer. (Answer in 250 words) 15
18. The Right of Children to Free and Compulsory Education Act, 2009 remains inadequate in promoting incentive-based system for children's education without generating awareness about the importance of schooling. Analyse. (Answer in 250 words) 15
19. How will I2U2 (India, Israel, UAE and USA) grouping transform India's position in global politics? (Answer in 250 words) 15
20. 'Clean energy is the order of the day.' Describe briefly India's changing policy towards climate change in various international fora in the context of geopolitics. (Answer in 250 words) 15

MAIN EXAMINATION—2022

General Studies Paper-III

1. Why is Public Private Partnership (PPP) required in infrastructural projects? Examine the role of PPP model in the redevelopment of Railway Stations in India. (Answer in 150 words) 10

2. Is inclusive growth possible under market economy? State the significance of financial inclusion in achieving economic growth in India. (Answer in 150 words) 10

3. What are the major challenges of Public Distribution System (PDS) in India? How can it be made effective and transparent? (Answer in 150 words) 10

4. Elaborate the scope and significance of the food processing industry in India. (Answer in 150 words) 10

5. The increase in life expectancy in the country has led to newer health challenges in the community. What are those challenges and what steps need to be taken to meet them? (Answer in 150 words) 10

6. Each year a large amount of plant material, cellulose, is deposited on the surface of Planet Earth. What are the natural processes this cellulose undergoes before yielding carbon dioxide, water and other end products? (Answer in 150 words) 10

7. Discuss in detail the photochemical smog emphasising its formation, effects and mitigation. Explain the 1999 Gothenburg Protocol. (Answer in 150 words) 10

8. Explain the mechanism and occurrence of cloudburst in the context of the Indian subcontinent. Discuss two recent examples. (Answer in 150 words) 10

9. Discuss the types of organised crimes. Describe the linkages between terrorists and organised crime that exist at the national and transnational levels. (Answer in 150 words) 10

10. What are the maritime security challenges in India ? Discuss the organisational, technical and procedural initiatives taken to improve the maritime security. (Answer in 150 words) 10

11. "Economic growth in the recent past has been led by increase in labour activity." Explain this statement. Suggest the growth pattern that will lead to creation of more jobs without compromising labour productivity. (Answer in 250 words) 15

12. Do you think India will meet 50 per cent of its energy needs from renewable energy by 2030? Justify your answer. How will the shift of subsidies from fossil fuels to renewables help achieve the above objective? Explain. (Answer in 250 words) 15

13. What are the main bottlenecks in upstream and downstream process of marketing of agricultural products in India? (Answer in 250 words) 15

14. What is Integrated Farming System? How is it helpful to small and marginal farmers in India? (Answer in 250 words) 15

15. Launched on 25th December, 2021, James Webb Space Telescope has been much in the news since then. What are its unique features which make it superior to its predecessor Space Telescopes? What are the key goals of this mission? What potential benefits does it hold for the human race? (Answer in 250 words) 15

16. What is the basic principle behind vaccine development? How do vaccines work? What approaches were adopted by the Indian vaccine manufacturers to produce COVID-19 vaccines? (Answer in 250 words) 15

17. Discuss global warming and mention its effects on the global climate. Explain the control measures to bring down the level of greenhouse gases which cause global warming, in the light of the Kyoto Protocol, 1997. (Answer in 250 words) 15

18. Explain the causes and effects of coastal erosion in India. What are the available coastal management techniques for combating the hazard? (Answer in 250 words) 15

19. What are the different elements of cyber security? Keeping in view the challenges in cyber security, examine the extent to which India has successfully developed a comprehensive National Cyber Security Strategy. (Answer in 250 words) 15

20. Naxalism is a social, economic and developmental issue manifesting as a violent internal security threat. In this context, discuss the emerging issues gest a multilayered strategy to tackle the menace of Naxalism. (Answer in 250 words) 15

MAIN EXAMINATION – 2022
General Studies Paper-IV

SECTION: A

1.(a) Wisdom lies in knowing what to reckon with and what to overlook. An officer being engrossed with the periphery, ignoring the core issues before him, is no rare in the bureaucracy. Do you agree that such preoccupation of an administrator leads to travesty of justice to the cause of effective service delivery and good governance? Critically evaluate. (Answer in 150 words) 10

(b) Apart from intellectual competency and moral qualities, empathy and compassion are some of the other vital attributes that facilitate the civil servants to be more competent in tackling the crucial issues or taking critical decisions. Explain with suitable illustrations. (Answer in 150 words) 10

2. (a) The Rules and Regulations provided to all the civil servants are same, yet there is difference in the performance. Positive minded officers are able to interpret the Rules and Regulations in favour of the case and achieve success, whereas negative minded officers are unable to achieve goals by interpreting the same Rules and Regulations against the case. Discuss with illustrations. (Answer in 150 words) 10

(b) It is believed that adherence to ethics in human actions would ensure in smooth functioning of an organisation/system. If so, what does ethics seek to promote in human life? How do ethical values assist in the resolution of conflicts faced by him in his day-to-day functioning? (Answer in 150 words) 10

3.(a) 'Ethics is knowing the difference between what you have the right to do and what is right to do.'– Potter Stewart (Answer in 150 words) 10

(b) "If a country is to be corruption free and become a nation of beautiful minds, I strongly feel there are three key societal members who can make a difference. They are the father, the mother and the teacher." – Abdul Kalam (Answer in 150 words) 10

(c) "Judge your success by what you had to give up in order to get it." – Dalai Lama. (Answer in 150 words) 10

4. (a) What do you understand by term 'good governance'? How far recent initiatives in terms of e-Governance steps taken by the State have helped the beneficiaries? Discuss with suitable examples. (Answer in 150 words) 10

(b) Online methodology is being used for day-to-day meetings, institutional approvals in the administration and for teaching and learning in education sector to the extent telemedicine in the health sector is getting popular with the approvals of the competent authority. No doubt it has advantages and disadvantages for both the beneficiaries and system at large. Describe and discuss the ethical issues involved in the use of online method particularly to vulnerable section of society. (Answer in 150 words) 10

5. (a) Russia and Ukraine war has been going on for the last seven months. Different countries have taken independent stands and actions keeping in view their own national interests. We are all aware that war has its own impact on the different aspects of society, including human tragedy. What are those ethical issues that are crucial to be considered while launching the war and its continuation so far? Illustrate with justification the ethical issues involved in the given state of affair. (Answer in 150 words) 10

(b) Write short notes on the following in 30 words each:

(i) Constitutional morality

(ii) Conflict of interest

(iii) Probity in public life

(iv) Challenges of digitalisation

(v) Devotion to duty

6.(a) Whistle blower, who reports corruption and illegal activities, wrongdoing and misconduct to the concerned authorities, runs the risk of being exposed to grave danger, physical harm and victimisation by the vested interests, accused persons and his team. What policy measures would you suggest to strengthen protection mechanism to safeguard the whistle blower? (Answer in 150 words) 10

(b) In contemporary world, corporate sector's contribution in generating wealth and employment is increasing. In doing so, they are bringing in unprecedented onslaught on the climate, environmental sustainability and living conditions of human beings. In this background, do you think Corporate Social Responsibility (CSR) is efficient and sufficient enough to fulfill the social roles and responsibilities needed in the corporate work mandated? Critically examine. (Answer in 150 words) 10

SECTION: B

7. Prabhat was working as Vice President (Marketing) at Sterling Electric Ltd., a reputed multinational company. But presently the company was passing through the difficult times as the sales were continuously showing downward trend in the last two quarters. His division, which hitherto had been a major revenue contributor to the company's financial health, was now desperately trying to procure some big government order for them. But their best efforts did not yield any positive success or breakthrough.

His was a professional company and his local bosses were under pressure from their London-based HO to show some positive results. In the last performance review meeting taken by the Executive Director (India Head), he was reprimanded for his poor performance. He assured them that his division is working on a special contract from the Ministry of Defence for a secret installation near Gwalior and tender is being submitted shortly.

He was under extreme pressure and he was deeply perturbed. What aggravated the situation further was a warning from the top that if the deal is not clinched in favour of the company, his division might have to be closed and he may have to quit his lucrative job.

There was another dimension which was causing him deep mental torture and agony. This pertained to his personal precarious financial health. He was a single earner in the family with two school-college going children and his old ailing mother. The heavy expenditure on education and medical was causing a big strain to his monthly pay packet. Regular EMI for housing loan taken from bank unavoidable and any default would render him liable for severe legal action.

In the above backdrop, he was hoping for some miracle to happen. There was sudden turn of events. His Secretary informed that a gentleman Subhas Verma wanted to see him as he was interested in the position of Manager which was to be filled by him in the company. He further brought to his notice that his CV has been received through the office of the Minister of Defence.

During interview of the candidate—Subhash Verma, he found him technically sound, resourceful and experienced marketeer. He seemed to be well-conversant with tendering procedures and having knack of follow-up and liaising in this regard Prabhat felt that he was better choice than the rest of the candidates who were recently interviewed by him in the last few days.

Subhash Verma also indicated that he was in possession of the copies of the bid documents that the Unique Electronics Ltd. would be submitting the next day to the Defence Ministry for their tender. He offered to hand over those documents subject to his employment in the company on suitable terms and conditions. He made it clear that in the process, the Sterling Electric Ltd. could outbid their rival company and get the bid and hefty Defence Ministry order. He indicated that it will be win-win situation for both—him and the company.

Prabhat was absolutely stunned. It was a mixed feeling of shock and thrill. He was uncomfortable and perspiring. If accepted, all his problems would vanish instantly and he may be rewarded for securing the much awaited tender and thereby boosting company's sales and financial health. He was in a fix as to the future course of action. He was wonder-struck at the guts of Subhash Verma in having surreptitiously removing his own company papers and offering to the rival company for a job. Being an experienced person, he was examining the pros and cons of the proposal/situation and he asked him to come the next day.

(a) Discuss the ethical issues involved in the case.

(b) Critically examine the options available to Prabhat in the above situation.

(c) Which of the above would be the most appropriate for Prabhat and why? (Answer in 250 words) 20

8. Ramesh is State Civil Services Officer who got the opportunity of getting posted to the capital of a border State after rendering 20 years of service. Ramesh's mother has recently been detected cancer and has been admitted in the leading cancer hospital of the city. His two adolescent children have also got admission in one of the best public schools of the town. After settling down in his appointment as Director in the Home Department of the State, Ramesh got confidential report through intelligence sources that illegal migrants are infiltrating in the State from the neighbouring country. He decided to personally carry out surprise check of the border posts along with his Home Department team. To his surprise, he caught red-handed two families of 12 members infiltrated with the connivance of the security personnel at the border posts. On further inquiry and investigation, it was found that after the migrants from

neighbouring country infiltrate, their documentation like Aadhaar Card, Ration Card and Voter Card are also forged and they are made to settle down in a particular area of the State. Ramesh prepared the detailed and comprehensive report and submitted to the Additional Secretary of the State. However, he was summoned by the Additional Home Secretary after a week and was instructed to withdraw the report. The Additional Home Secretary informed Ramesh that the report submitted by him has not been appreciated by the higher authorities. He further cautioned him that if he fails to withdraw the confidential report, he will not only be posted out from the prestigious appointment from the State capital but his further promotion which is due in near future will also get in jeopardy.

(a) What are the options available to Ramesh as the Director of the Home Department of the bordering State?

(b) What option should Ramesh adopt and why?

(c) Critically evaluate each of the options.

(d) What are the ethical dilemmas being faced by Ramesh?

(e) What policy measures would you suggest to combat the menace of infiltration of illegal migrants from the neighbouring country?

(Answer in 250 words) 20

9. The Supreme Court has banned mining in the Aravalli Hills to stop degradation of the forest cover and to maintain ecological balance. However, the stone mining is still prevalent in the border district of the affected State with connivance of certain corrupt forest officials and politicians. Young and dynamic SP who was recently posted in the affected district promised to himself to stop this menace. In one of his surprise checks with his team, he found loaded truck with stone trying to escape the mining area. He tried to stop the truck but

the truck driver overrun the police officer, killing him on the spot and thereafter managed to flee. Police filed FIR but no breakthrough was achieved in the case for almost three months. Ashok who was the Investigative Journalist working with leading TV channel, suo moto started investigating the case. Within one month, Ashok got breakthrough by interacting with local people, stone mining mafia and government officials. He prepared his investigative story and presented to the CMD of the TV channel. He exposed in his investigative report the complete nexus of stone mafia working with blessing of corrupt police and civil officials and politicians. The politician who was involved in the mafia was no one else but local MLA who was considered to be very close to the Chief Minister. After going through the investigative report, the CMD advised Ashok to drop the idea of making the story public through electronic media. He informed that the local MLA was not only the relative of the owner of the TV channel but also had unofficially 20 per cent share in the channel. The CMD further informed Ashok that his further promotion and hike in pay will be taken care of in addition to the soft loan of 10 lakhs which he has taken from the TV channel for his son's chronic disease will be suitably adjusted if he hands over the investigative report to him.

(a) What are the options available with Ashok to cope up with the situation?

(b) Critically evaluate/examine each of the options identified by Ashok.

(c) What are the ethical dilemmas being faced by Ashok?

(d) Which of the options, do you think, would be the most appropriate for Ashok to adopt and why?

(e) In the above scenario, what type of training would you suggest for police officers posted to such districts where illegal activities like stone mining are rampant? (Answer in 250 words) 20

10. You have done MBA from a reputed institution three years back but could not get campus placement due to COVID-19-generated recession. However, after a lot of persuasion and series of competitive tests including written and interview, you managed to get a job in a leading shoe company. You have aging parents who are dependent and staying with you. You also recently got married after getting this decent job. You were allotted the Inspection Section which is responsible for clearing the final product. In first one year, you learnt your job well and was appreciated for your performance by the management. The company is doing good business for last five years in domestic market and this year it is decided even to export to Europe and Gulf countries. However, one large consignment to Europe was rejected by their Inspecting Team due to certain poor quality and was sent back. The top management ordered that ibid. consignment to be cleared for the domestic market. As a part of Inspecting Team, you observed the glaring poor quality and brought to the knowledge of the Team Commander. However, the top management advised all the members of the team to overlook these defects as the management cannot bear such a huge loss. Rest of the team members except you promptly signed and cleared the consignment for domestic market, overlooking glaring defects. You again brought to the knowledge of the Team Commander that such consignment, if cleared even for domestic market, will tarnish the image and reputation of the company and will be counter-productive in the long run. However, you were further advised by the top management that if you do not clear the consignment, the company will not hesitate to terminate your services citing certain innocuous reasons.

    (a) Under the given conditions, what are the options available to you as a member of the Inspecting Team?

(b) Critically evaluate each of the options listed by you.

(c) What option would you adopt and why?

(d) What are the ethical dilemmas being faced by you?

(e) What can be the consequences of overlooking the observations raised by the Inspecting Team?

(Answer in 250 words) 20

11. Rakesh was working as a Joint Commissioner in Transport department of a city. As a part of his job profile, among others, he was entrusted with the task of overseeing the control and functioning of City Transport Department. A case strike by drivers' union of City Transport Department over the issue of compensation to a driver who died on duty while driving the bus came up before him for decision in the matter.

He gathered that the driver (deceased) was plying Bus No. 528 which passed through busy and congested roads of the city. It so happened that near an intersection on the way, there was an accident involving a middle-aged man. It was found that there was altercation between the driver and the car driver. Heated arguments between them led to a fight and the driver gave him a blow. A lot of passersby had gathered and tried to intervene but without success. Eventually, both of them were badly injured and profusely bleeding and were taken to the nearby hospital. The driver succumbed to the injuries and could not be saved. The middle-aged driver's condition was also critical but after a day, he recovered and was discharged. Police had immediately come to the spot and FIR was registered. Police investigation revealed that the quarrel was started by the bus driver and he had resorted to physical violence. There was exchange of blows between them.

The City Transport Department management is considering of not giving any extra compensation to the driver's (deceased) family. The family is very aggrieved, depressed and agitated against the discriminatory and non-sympathetic approach of the City Transport Department management. The bus driver (deceased) was 52 years of age, was survived by his wife and two school-college going daughters. He was the sole earner of the family. The City Transport Department workers' union took up this case and when found no favourable response from the management, decided to go on strike. The union's demand was two fold. First was full compensation as given to other drivers who died on duty and secondly employment to one family member. The strike has continued for 10 days and the deadlock remains.

(a) What are the options available to Rakesh to meet the above situation?

(b) Critically examine each of the options identified by Rakesh.

(c) What are the ethical dilemmas being faced by Rakesh?

(d) What course of action would Rakesh adopt to diffuse the above situation?

(Answer in 250 words) 20

12. You are appointed as an officer heading the section in Environment Pollution Control Board to ensure compliance and its follow-up. In that region, there were a large number of small and medium industries which had been granted clearance. You learnt that these industries provide employment to many migrant workers. Most of the industrial units have got environmental clearance certificate in their possession. The environmental clearance seeks to curb industries and projects that supposedly hamper environment and living species in the region. But in practice, most of these units remain to be polluting units in several ways like air, water and soil pollution. As such, local people encountered persistent health problems.

It was confirmed that majority of the industries were violating environmental compliance. You issued notice to all the industrial units to apply for fresh environmental clearance certificate from the competent authority. However, your action met with hostile response from a section of the industrial units, other vested interest persons and a section of the local politicians. The workers also became hostile to you as they felt that your action would lead to the closure of these industrial units, and the resultant unemployment will lead to insecurity and uncertainty in their livelihood. Many owners of the industries approached you with the plea that you should not initiate harsh action as it would compel them to shut their units, and cause huge financial losses, as well as shortage of their products in the market. These would obviously add to the suffering of the labourers and the consumers alike. The labour union also sent you representation requesting against the closure of the units. You simultaneously started receiving threats from unknown corners. You however received supports from some of your colleagues, who advised you to act freely to ensure environmental compliance. Local NGOs also came to your support and they demanded the closure of the polluting units immediately.

(a) What are the options available to you under the given situation?

(b) Critically examine the options listed by you.

(c) What type of mechanism would you suggest to ensure environmental compliance?

(d) What are the ethical dilemmas you faced in exercising your option?

(Answer in 250 words) 20

❑

200 Motivational Quotes

1. A person who is nice to you, but rude to the waiter, is not a nice person.

   —Dave Barry

2. Never miss an opportunity to make others happy, even if you have to leave them alone in order to do it.

   —Anonymous

3. Getting money is not all a man's business: to cultivate kindness is a valuable part of the business of life.

   —Samuel Johnson

4. If we cannot be clever, we can always be kind.

   —Alfred Fripp

5. I always prefer to believe the best of everybody, it saves so much trouble.

   — Rudyard Kipling

6. No act of kindness, however small, is ever wasted.

   —Aesop

7. It is not length of life, but depth of life.

   —Ralph Waldo Emerson

8. A creative man is motivated by the desire to achieve, not by the desire to beat others.

   —Ayn Rand

9. If life is a race, chasing your dream should be your aim, not competing with others.

   —Blaze Olamiday

10. That best portion of a good man's life; his little, nameless, unremembered acts of kindness and love.

—William Wordsworth

11. Better to light one small candle than to curse the darkness.

—Chinese Proverb

12. The secret of success is making your vocation your vacation.

—Mark Twain

13. The heart and soul of a company is creativity and innovation.

—Robert Iger

14. Hardships are motivating forces which test a man and make him move ahead.

—Damodar Vinayak Sawarkar

15. Hurdles are a man's test. They should enhance up your enthusiasm, not diminish it.

—Yashpal

16. Speaking about oneself often becomes difficult, because it is unpleasant for one to see one's own weaknesses and difficult for others to overlook them.

—Mahadevi Verma

17. Like the world is dark for the blind and is bright for those who can see, likewise it is full of sorrow for the ignorant and full of happiness for the knowledgeable.

—Sampurnananda

18. Great mind discuss ideas. Average mind discuss events. Small minds discuss people.

—Eleanor Roosevelt

19. Work spares us from three evils: boredom, vice, and need.

—Voltaire

20. He emerges victorious who takes risk to get his work done. Cowards can never be victorious.

—Jawaharlal Nehru

21. The scent of a flower never flows against the wind, but the fragrance of a person's virtues spreads all around.

—Gautam Buddha

22. Any work done by you may have no value, but it is important that you do something.

—Mahatma Gandhi

23. High expectations are the key to absolutely everything.

—Sam Walton

24. Books are teachers which teach us without giving any botheration, without criticising and without testing us.

—Ganesh Shankar Vidyarthi

25. Blind people do not see the world, lusty have no conscience, drunkards think they are most superior and the selfish people see no wrong.

—Acharya Chanakya

26. Nature is a limitless reservoir of knowledge. There is a lesson in every leaf, but to take advantage of it, one needs experience.

—Ayodhya Singh Upadhyay 'Hariaudh'

27. Work does not require much effort, but it takes much more effort to decide what to do.

—Unknown

28. No man can be successful, unless he first loves his work.

—David Sarnoff

29. In a class, a new student does not bring anything and an old student takes nothing away, but still knowledge flourishes.

—Rajendra Awasthi

30. The Goddess of Wealth 'Lakshmi' blesses those who bless others.

—Sudarshan

31. Challenge yourself with something you know you could never do, and what you'll find is that you can overcome anything.

—Anonymous

32. "Of course motivation is not permanent. But then, neither is bathing; but it is something you should do on a regular basis."

—Zig Ziglar

33. Success consists of doing the common thing of life uncommonly well.

—George Washington

34. It is easy to be victorious over a thousand soldiers, but one who wins over himself, is truly victorious.

—Gautam Buddha

35. Do not stop for plucking and picking flowers. Keep moving ahead, flowers will keep blooming in your path.

—Rabindranath Tagore

36. Wealth is created by good deeds, grows by boldness (courage, capability and determination), blossoms by ingenuity and is secured by self-control.

—Mahatma Bidur

37. The knowledgeable learn by wisdom, the common man by experience, the ignorant by necessity and animals by nature.

—Acharya Kautilya

38. Education without character, science without humanity and trade without ethics are dangerous.

—Satya Sai Baba

39. You are definitely rewarded for your thoughts and work. Good for good and bad for bad. This is the law of nature. It could be delayed, but is bound to happen. So, if you want to be successful, nurture good thoughts, perform good deeds and serve-help the needy selflessly. Do not be disturbed by difficulties, hurdles and criticism which you come across.

—Swett Marden

40. Just as the Sun's image does not form on a dusty mirror, similarly a blemished conscience cannot be illuminated by God.

—Ramakrishna Paramahansa

41. Just as the darkness of the night can only be cleared by the Sun, man's crisis can only be removed by knowledge.

—Narad Bhakti

42. Hardship and crisis are the best educators of a man. Those who face them with courage emerge victorious.

—Lokmanya Tilak

43. Strength does not come from physical capacity. It comes from an indomitable will.

—Mahatma Gandhi

44. Justice and morality are the toys of Mother Lakshmi. She makes you dance as she desires.

—Premchand

45. Howsoever pure your propositions may be, you cannot achieve them without the purity of the means of attainment.

—Kamlapati Tripathi

46. "Fear doesn't shut you down; it wakes you up. I've seen it. It's fascinating." He releases me but doesn't pull away, his hand grazing my jaw, my neck. "Sometimes I just...want to see it again. Want to see you awake."

—Veronica Roth

47. If opportunity doesn't knock, build a door.

—Milton Berle

48. Hard work removes poverty, religion removes sins, silence removes conflicts and remaining awake removes fear.

—Acharya Chanakya

49. Just as sunshine removes darkness, similarly happiness of the mind removes all hurdles.

—Amritlal Nagar

50. We should be taught not to wait for inspiration to start a thing. Action always generates inspiration. Inspiration seldom generates action.

—Frank Tibolt

51. Mistakes are part of learning knowledge. If you make a mistake, do not ponder over it for too long. Learn from it and move ahead. You can't change the past. The future is still in your hands.

—Sukrat

52. I do not consider my life a profession. I believe in work. I learn from circumstances. This is not a profession or a job, it is the essence of life.

—Steve Jobs

53. Focus on one objective only. Do not divert your attention till you achieve the objective. Day and night keep it in your mind, even dream about it. Only then shall you attain success.

—Swami Vivekananda

54. Well done is better than well said.

—Benjamin Franklin

55. A king's happiness lies in the happiness of his people, and in their welfare only should the king consider his welfare. Self-praise is not in his interest but the praise by his people is in his interest.

—Acharya Chanakya

56. Sobriety is the basis of culture. Indulgence, weakness and flattery neither lead to emergence of culture nor its development.

—Kaka Kalelkar

57. The tree of patience is bitter, but bears sweet fruits.

—Swami Shivananda

58. "It's not the load that breaks you down, it's the way you carry it.

—Lou Hotz

59. The seeds of good deed sown at the right place bear great fruits.

—Katha Saritsagar

60. If discontentment is not converted into a constructive force by dint of dedication and patience, it can be dangerous.

—Indira Gandhi

61. The best teachers are those who tells you where to look, but don't tell what to see.

—Alexandra K. Trenfor

62. Setting goals is the first step in turning the invisible into visible.

—Tony Robbins

63. Knowing is not enough; we must apply. Willing is not enough; we must do.

—Bruce Lee

64. Nothing great was ever achieved without enthusiasm.

—Ralph Waldo Emerson

65. Happy are those who dream dreams and are ready to pay the price to make them come true.

—Leon J. Suenes

66. Along with success comes a reputation for wisdom.

—Euripides

67. The surest way not to fail is to determine to succeed.

—Richard Brinsley Sheridan

68. Careful thinking and hard work will solve nearly all your problems. Try and see for yourself.

—Ullery

69. A tree bows when it bears fruit, the clouds bow when it rains and a gentleman becomes modest when he has wealth. Such is the nature of people who help others.

—Goswami Tulsidas

70. Just as repudiation of death is necessary to live, similarly one must repudiate prestige to remain creative.

—Dr. Raghuvansh

71. The purpose of literature is not just to impart knowledge, but to provide a new atmosphere as well.

—Dr. Sarvepalli Radhakrishnan

72. Not to be disappointed is the basis of success and this is the ultimate happiness.

—Maharishi Valmiki

73. For attaining eternal peace, one need not desire peace, but suppression of all desires.

—Swami Gyanananda

74. You are never too old to set another goal or to dream a new dream.

—C.S. Lewis

75. Punishment must be used as a deterrent to protect people, but punishment must not be given without reason.

—Shri Ramayana

76. After extreme happiness and excessive progress comes the turn of extreme sadness and downfall.

—Jaishankar Prasad

77. The plant of democracy, of any sort, cannot flourish in a dictatorship.

—Loknayak Jaiprakash Narayan

78. Life becomes important only when it is devoted for a great cause. Such devotion should be based on justice and knowledge.

—Indira Gandhi

79. Man can win over anger by love, sin by righteousness, greed by charity and falsehood by truth.

—Gautam Buddha

80. Lethargy is the greatest enemy of man and hard work is his best friend and one who stays with it is never sad.

—Bhartrihari

81. The three pillars of knowledge—more experience, more patience and more study.

—Unknown

82. Difficulties are the test for mankind. No one can become successful without passing this test.

—Pandit Rampratap Tripathi

83. Just like a blade of grass shows the direction of the wind, similarly minor incidents show the nature of the human heart.

—Mahatma Gandhi

84. Two kinds of people fail—those who think but do not act and those who act without thinking.

—Acharya Sriram Sharma

85. The more a man becomes educated, the more he becomes involved in work.

—Vinoba Bhave

86. Neglect of the general public is a national crime.

—Swami Vivekananda

87. People, who do not put in effort, do not attain wealth, friends, happiness, health, peace and satisfaction.

—Ved Vyasa

88. Just as we use water to douse fire, similarly we must use knowledge to calm our mind.

—Ved Vyasa

89. A moon spreads its light in the entire sky, but keeps its blemish to itself.

—Rabindranath Tagore

90. There are three jewels on earth—water, food and softly-spoken words. However, the ignorant considers a piece of stone to be a jewel.

—Mahakavi Kalidasa

91. Falsehood is like a stack of hay. A spark of truth can reduce it to ashes.

—Haribhau Upadhaya

92. Instead of flying high, when we bow, we become wiser.

—Unknown

93. Iron may become hot, but a hammer works even when it is cold.

—Sardar Patel

94. Till today nothing great has been achieved without great enthusiasm.

—Netaji Subhash Chandra Bose

95. Dreams don't always come true, but life remains pivoted on hope.

—Ravikiran Shastri

96. A tree bears heat, but its shade cools down others.

—Goswami Tulsidas

97. To turn away from righteousness and indulge in notorious activity is bad, but someone talking pleasantly on your face and then back-stabbing is worse.

—Sant Thiruvalluvar

98. Every work happens in its own time. It serves no purpose to be impatient. No matter how much you water a tree, it will bear fruits only when it is time.

—Vrinda

99. Flattery does not harm you until you accept it as the truth.

—Premchand

100. To be human is in itself a victory for a human, to be a demon is his defeat and to be a demigod is a miracle.

—Dr. Sarvepalli Radhakrishnan

101. Absence of light is not the only darkness; too much of it also blinds the eye.

—Swami Ramteerth

102. Even the sea breaks all boundaries when there is a storm, but gentlemen maintain their dignity even during a serious crisis.

—Chanakya

103. Books show the way like a beacon in the ocean of time.

—Unknown

104. It is true that one who swims, drowns, and not the one standing on the shore. However, the latter never learns to swim either.

—Vallabhbhai Patel

105. Worship and faith are such herbs which, if someone consumes, can wish away death.

—Amritlal Nagar

106. At the age of 20, a man's appearance is the gift of nature, at age of 30, it is the gift of the vagaries of life, but the appearance at the age of 50 is his own earning.

—Ashtavakra

107. The way to a better life is through good books.

—Shilpayan

108. Anyone who loves to read books can remain happy anywhere.

—Mahatma Gandhi

109. We may not be able to reach the stars, but we can set our sight towards them.

—Jawaharlal Nehru

110. Anyone who feels scared by the thought of defeat is definitely defeated.

—Napolean

111. My message to the youth is in three words—work, work, work.

—Bismarck

112. Even if you fall on your face, you're still moving forward.

—Victor Kiam

113. Possible asks impossible—"Where do you live?"

Impossible replies—"In the dreams of the weak."

—Rabindranath Tagore

114. If you stay dependent on destiny, it will continue to sleep. If you rise with courage, your destiny will also rise.

—Unknown

115. Set an aim for your life, then devote all your physical and mental strength which God has given you, in achieving that aim.

—Carlyle

116. Only he is untouched by failure, who has never tried.

—Whitley

117. Beware of a flatterer, he is a great thief. He will fool you and steal your time and intellect.

—Chanakya

118. Start where you are. Use what you have. Do what you can.

—Arthur Ashe

119. Howsoever short life may be, it is further shortened by wasting time.

—Johnson

120. Everyone waits for time, but only the intelligent take advantage of it.

—Umashankar

121. Whatever your mind wills starts happening.

—Acharya Rajneesh

122. Success is attained by wisdom and hard work. If you want to rise, then adopt both.

—Mahakavi Magh

123. Nothing is impossible for anyone who takes a vow and pursues it. It is the key to success.

—Morabi

124. To educate children is necessary, but it is also necessary to let them educate themselves.

—Ernest Dimnet

125. Education is above all other achievements in the world.

—Suryakant Tripathi 'Nirala'

126. If we learn from failure, then it is indeed a success.

—Malcolm Forbes

127. "Every day People straighten up the hair, why not the heart?"

—Ernesto Guevara

128. If one wants to learn, then each mistake can teach him something.

—Mahatma Gandhi

129. Education that makes one narrow-minded and selfish, no matter what value it might have had earlier, has no value today.

—Sharat Chandra Chattopadhyay

130. Whomsoever I meet is superior to me in some respect. So, I learn something from him.

—Emerson

131. Winning isn't everything, but wanting to win is.

—Vince Lombardi

132. O powerful guide! Bestow upon us the best knowledge by using your protection power and multifaceted power of education. Relieve us from vices, hunger and diseases.

—Rig Veda

133. Though the whole world longs for freedom, yet every creature loves its attachments. This is the first complexity and contradiction of nature.

—Shri Aurobindo

134. The truthful issues are the same for everyone; conflict happens on account of untrue issues.

—Satyarth Prakash

135. One must have faith in Guru or God, because without faith, everything is meaningless.

—Samarth Guru Ramdas

136. Hatred cannot be destroyed by hatred. We can end it by the power of love.

—Sant Vinoba Bhave

137. You may be disappointed if you fail, but you are doomed if you don't try.

—Beverly Sills

138. Patience and wisdom are as much necessary for parliamentary democracy as are balance and decorous consciousness.

—Dr. Shankar Dayal Sharma

139. In order to succeed, your desire for success should be greater than your fear of failure."

—Bill Cosby

140. It is better to die while praying, than to be victorious by committing sin.

—Mahabharata

141. Those who stay ahead of the lamp, cast their own shadow in their path.

—Rabindranath Tagore

142. Nature, time and patience—these three are the cures for every pain.

—Sant Gyaneshwar

143. Knowledge is an ornament in good times, an assistant in bad times and saved wealth during old age.

—Hitopadesh

144. One who can listen to music amid chaos, achieves great heights.

—Dr. Vikram Sarabhai

145. To quarrel without reason is a sign of foolishness. So, the wise thing to do is to bear your loss and not get into an argument.

—Hitopadesh

146. No one can make you feel inferior without your consent.

—Eleanor Roosevelt

147. The snake has poison in its fangs, the fly in its head and the scorpion in its tail, but evil people have poison in their entire body.

—Sant Kabir

148. No plan will be successful in a nation which does not possess character.

—Vinoba Bhave

149. The liberal-minded look for truth in different religions. The narrow-minded only look for differences.

—A Chinese proverb

150. Conscience is the salt of life and imagination its sweetness. One preserves life and the other makes it sweet.

—Unknown

151. There are sweet streams even inside rocks. Cold water, not wine, flows through them.

—Jaishankar Prasad

152. What you learn in the school of experience cannot be learnt from books and universities.

—Unknown

153. Just like a small breeze can stoke a fire, similarly a little effort can alter your destiny.

—Unknown

154. A truthful person, even if he is not a scholar, can do a lot of service for his country.

—Pandit Motilal Nehru

155. "It is the mark of an educated mind to be able to entertain a thought without accepting it."

—Aristotle

156. Just like an owl cannot see the Sun, similarly an evil person cannot see gentleness.

—Swami Bhajnananda

157. Your mind is a cowardly enemy, which always attacks you from behind.

—Premchand

158. Don't complain; just work harder.

—Randy Pausch

159. Time is the wealth of change, but the clock only shows it in the form of change, not in the form of wealth.

—Rabindranath Tagore

160. While studying, put the entire world aside and immerse yourself in books, authors and their views. This is your meditation. This is your worship and your prayer as well.

—Pandit Madan Mohan Malviya

161. We laugh at jokes on others, but forget even to cry if the joke is on us.

—Acharya Ramchandra Shukla

162. What work buckets of water can't do is done by merely two drops of medicine and what the sword can't do is done by a thorn.

—Sudarshan

163. Electric light may dispel some darkness, but it cannot replace the Sun. Similarly, a foreign language cannot work like a Sun. The progress of the country and development of its literature can only be achieved by a country's own language.

—Pandit Madan Mohan Malviya

164. The greatest victory is of love which binds the hearts of the victorious forever.

—Samrat Ashok

165. The general of an immoral army is lie. Wherever lie treads, there an immoral state's victory bigule definitely sounds.

—Sudarshan

166. The main use of the wealth of great people is to ease the hardships from the lives of other people.

—Rahim Das

167. Education is at the root of all improvements.

—Pandit Madan Mohan Malviya

168. People who try never lose.

—Harivansh Rai Bachchan

169. One who hordes wealth does not know the value of charity.

—Acharya Sriram Sharma

170. Whether you want to live in Satyug (righteous times) or Kaliyug (evil times) is for you to decide. You hold your own yug (time).

—Vinoba Bhave

171. The number of people who die of overeating is much greater than the number of people who die of hunger.

—A proverb

172. Wealth can be repaid, but word of sympathy is a debt, repayment of which is beyond man's power.

—Sudarshan

173. Remain modest at all times. Modesty is what makes a human truly human. Modesty is a man's greatest asset.

—Pandit Madan Mohan Malviya

174. The penalty for being famous is that one needs to progress constantly.

—Unknown

175. The fundamental principle of success of a democratic rule is that everyone behaves virtuously.

—Rajagopalachari

176. A woman's pity is the world's greatest evolvement on which all good deeds are based.

—Jaishankar Prasad

177. The moon, the Himalayas, the banana tree and sandalwood are all considered cool, but nothing is cooler than a human mind without any desires.

—Maharishi Vashishta

178. There are two things worthy of love in this universe—one is sorrow and the other is hard work. Without sorrow, the heart does not turn tender and without hard work, humaneness does not develop.

—Acharya Sriram Sharma

179. Only Hindi can help sustain the unity of the nation.

—Subramaniam Bharti

180. Disintegration leads to destruction, while integration leads to formation.

—Kanhaiyalal Mishra Prabhakar

181. Gentlemen, much like the clouds, accept anything only to give it away.

—Mahakavi Kalidas

182. There is only one infallible medicine to dispel sorrow—not to worry about it.

—Ved Vyas

183. Without scriptures, God is silent, justice is asleep, science is dazed and all other things are in complete darkness.

—Unknown

184. A revolutionary is not discouraged by defeat but his capability and dedication are enhanced.

—Mahatma Gandhi

185. English medium is the greatest bane of Indian education. In the civilised world for no other populace, the medium of education is a foreign language.

—Pandit Madan Mohan Malviya

186. A jolly person is like a spray whose droplets lighten everyone's heart.

—Unknown

187. The source of our happiness lies within us. It flourishes when we sympathise with others.

—Dalai Lama

188. Spring is pleasant. Summer is also pleasant. Monsoon, autumn and winter are also pleasant. This means that every time is a good time.

—Sama Veda

189. There is fear of disease in material pleasure, downfall in high caste, wealth loss for a king, insult in esteem, enemy in strength, old age in beauty and controversy in Shastras (scriptures). Only detachment is fearless.

—Lord Mahavira

190. There are no friends or enemies. Your behaviour creates friends and foes.

—Hitopadesh

191. Suffering develops perspective, so self-suffering is the way to self-realisation.

—Lord Mahavira

192. The fire of hatred does not extinguish until it destroys one of the parties.

—Ved Vyasa

193. It is better to light a lamp instead of blaming darkness.

—Upanishad

194. Temporary adversity is good as it helps to identify friends and foes.

—Rahim

195. To live for a hundred years, one must forgo all such pleasures for which we want to live for a hundred years.

—Unknown

196. Gentlemen fulfil the wishes of others without being told, just as the Sun lights up the homes on its own.

—Mahakavi Kalidas

197. Just as a mirror is of no use to a blind, similarly education is of no use to a mindless person.

—Premchand

198. Time and wisdom can lighten the worst of shocks.

—A proverb

199. He is noble whose heart is full of compassion and faith, who speaks sweetly and whose eyes are filled with courtesy.

—Sant Malukdas

200. A fool can ask more questions in a minute than twelve wise men can answer in an hour.

—Swami Shivananda

❑❑❑